Across America on the Yellow Brick Road

Across America on the Yellow Brick Road

Cycling into a New Life

Virginia Mudd

Illustrations by Pat Edwards

SUNSTONE
PRESS

SANTA FE

Grateful acknowledgment is made for permission to reprint parts of the following:

I Whistle a Happy Tune by Rodgers & Hammerstein II, Copyright © 1951 by Richard Rodgers & Oscar Hammerstein II.

Williamson Music, Inc., owner of publication and allied rights for the Western Hemisphere and Japan; International Copyright secured; All rights reserved; used by permission.

Paradise by John Prine, Copyright © 1971 by Walden Music, Inc. and Sour Grapes Music. All rights reserved; used by permission.

The Impossible Dream by Joe Darion and Mitch Leigh, Copyright © 1965 by Andrew Scott, Inc. and Helena Music Corp.

All rights reserved; used by permission.

Sunstone books may be purchased for educational, business, or sales promotional use. For information please write: Special Markets Department, Sunstone Press, P.O. Box 2321, Santa Fe, New Mexico 87504-2321.

Illustrations by Pat Edwards
Book design › Vicki Ahl
Body typeface › Poliphilus MT Pro
Printed on acid-free paper
∞
eBook 978-1-61139-356-9

Library of Congress Cataloging-in-Publication Data

Mudd, Virginia, 1949-
Across America on the yellow brick road : cycling into a new life / by Virginia Mudd ; illustrations by Pat Edwards.
    pages cm
ISBN 978-1-63293-048-4 (softcover : alk. paper)
1. Mudd, Virginia, 1949- --Travel--United States. 2. United States--Description and travel. 3. Bicycle touring--United States. 4. Women cyclists--United States--Biography. 5. Cyclists--United States--Biography. I. Title.
E169.Z8M817 2015
917.304--dc23
                    2014044953

WWW.SUNSTONEPRESS.COM
SUNSTONE PRESS / POST OFFICE BOX 2321 / SANTA FE, NM 87504-2321 /USA
(505) 988-4418 / ORDERS ONLY (800) 243-5644 / FAX (505) 988-1025

To Gerry for his inspiration
To Linne for her guidance
To Tony for his encouragement
To Carol for a dream come true

Acknowledgements

To all the people across America who befriended us, thank you for your open hearts and many kindnesses. You rekindled my faith in the goodness of people.

And also my thanks to Shoshanna Alexander, my editor and project coordinator, for making possible the adventure of creating this book.

Contents

"It's a long journey through a country that is sometimes pleasant and sometimes dark and terrible."

—From The Wizard Of Oz by L. Frank Baum.

The Beginning

My life has been so short, that I really know nothing whatever.

I'm the last person I ever would have imagined to write a personal adventure story. The most adventuresome thing I did as a child was to ride my bike to the local shopping district a mile from my house, and that not until I was in the seventh grade and then only if I didn't ride through The Alley. Home was a rambling, stately brick house in a wealthy, but unglittery, area of Los Angeles. My parents and their families were prominent members of the community—patrons, directors and presidents of prestigious organizations—but they were careful to keep a low public profile. Mother was particularly fearful of the lucrative kidnapping possibilities presented by us five children, and she frequently recounted to me tales of domestic terror—armed men tricking the maid into opening the door, tying up the servants or locking them in a closet and making off with precious family jewels or children. I was trained to thoroughly distrust strangers, especially men offering ice cream cones (which never happened). My sister and I were not even allowed to camp out in our own backyard overnight. During the thirteen years I lived in Los Angeles, I didn't ride a city bus once. Thus was I carefully shepherded through childhood, knowing only the private worlds of my house, school, and one or two respectable areas of town.

This carefully planned and protected life continued through high school at an exclusive, all-girls' boarding school in Connecticut. My freedom and exposure to the outside world was limited to two weekends a year in New York City. After graduating, I followed my older sister Tory to Stanford University as I had followed her to boarding school. Within two months after my arrival, I had met a senior man on a blind date. It wasn't long before I was seen leaving my dorm in Tony's Lotus for the night, and soon I had moved off campus to live with him. Three days before my twentieth birthday, we were married.

Physically, I had been as incubated as I was socially and emotionally. Prenatal and infancy illnesses left me billed as physically handicapped through childhood. I was shuttled from one specialist to another for various neurological problems—an underdeveloped right side of my body, poor eyesight and circulation deficiencies. I was told I wasn't as strong as other children and had to nap in the afternoon years after my friends had stopped.

I was always last in sports, afraid to compete or even try, because I was so sure of failing. Gymnastics class in elementary school was torture. My turn would come, and I'd stand in front of the horse with an iron clamp in my stomach, fighting back tears and the urge to flee. After a lead-assed, klutzy effort to get through the exercise, I would slink away, thoroughly defeated and ashamed. My weakling self-image was intensified when I compared myself to Tory. She is lean, agile and graceful, and excelled in most school athletics. I "took after my mother," she told me—short, unathletic, with a "figure problem." The same person, ten years later, determined to ride a bicycle across America.

Along with the privileges of growing up rich came a sense of tremendous obligation and responsibility to serve the community, to repay the world for the undeserved, unearned abundance that was bestowed on me at birth. I didn't consciously realize the extent of this enormous sense of guilt until I was thirty; I only knew that when the first energy crisis came in 1973, followed two years later by the long California drought, I became a compulsive and fanatic conservationist. It took me several years of therapy and introspection to understand that, on a subconscious level, I felt the drought was my fault and that I had complete responsibility for saving gas—my own and everyone else's.

A short time before the long gas lines formed, I had bought a bicycle, along with thousands of Americans caught up in the bicycle craze. At first I rode for the novelty of it; then I rode to save gas. I prided myself, in those gas-precious months, on saving 150 gallons a year. Tony and I were living in the San Francisco Bay Area suburbs. He had his first job out of law school, and I was working for my recently-elected congressman. During his campaign, I got into the habit of delivering election materials and canvassing precincts on my bike, even in 100-degree weather. People were impressed. That recognition was good for my self-image, so I kept riding and conserving and carrying buckets of bathtub water to the garden. It became a way of life.

After three years on that first 10-speed, I had proven to myself that it was no longer just a fad, and I could justify buying a better model to make my transportation more efficient and pleasant. I got a silver and red Motobecane Grand Jubilee for $350 and felt I'd reached the height of professional biking. The bike was light as a feather, the wheels shiny, the tires thin. I proudly named it "Little Silver" and rode it everywhere I could.

The more I rode to fulfill my obligation to save energy, the more I came to enjoy bicycling in and of itself—the exercise, the speed that was all my own, the sense of independence and freedom. I was convinced that bicycling was the superior means of travel, by far the most energy-efficient mode of human transportation. I was so convinced that I sold our green Volvo sportswagon, a car we both loved driving, proclaiming it unnecessary. Everything I wanted or needed to do I could accomplish with my bike.

At some point during the height of my enthusiasm for biking, we received a postcard from a friend, Gerry Neville. He was somewhere in Minnesota en route from San Francisco to Boston by bicycle. Gerry had appeared during the construction of our handmade house to ask for a job. He had worked with us for several months, quiet, patient and meticulous in all his work. He was anything but a jock. The very idea of him bicycling across America was unbelievable. It set my head spinning with fantasies and dreams. If he could do it, so could I. I made a secret promise to myself, but the secret was too big to contain, and I found myself telling a few friends, "Someday I'm going to bicycle across the country." I was surprised by my own conviction. I didn't know how it would be done or with whom, just that it would certainly be accomplished. Time would reveal the means.

The first step toward my dream took place in April of 1977 when I made a trip to Chicago to attend a school for community organizers. I was excited about the prospect of taking the train all by myself to a strange city to do something just for me. It turned out to be an even more dramatic turning point in my life than I'd anticipated.

This was the first time I was making a trip alone since Tony and I had been married eight years before. When I arrived in Chicago I was almost overwhelmed by the insecurity of having no one to chaperone me, but I quickly gathered courage, for lack of a better alternative. I found myself easily making friends with the other people at the school. I was in my own world at last, talking not about Tony's interests as a lawyer, but about my own activities, ambitions and politics. My usual manner was to be shy and awkward, continually doubting my intelligence and worthiness among Tony and his eloquent colleagues. But here, to my surprise and delight, I found myself popular, outgoing and participating capably in discussions.

How fitting that I would have the opportunity for an affair. My attraction to the man was mild, the friendship developing in a relaxed, pleasant way during the first week. It was only when I found myself lying on my hotel bed next to him—both of us fully clothed, with his hand covering my breast and my body feeling as if it would explode—that I realized how much I wanted to have sex with him.

Never had I felt so stimulated. I couldn't believe that this lusting, aroused body was mine. I simply felt like a totally different person. Despite the temptation, the passion, the electric chemistry between us—and a classic bedroom drama—I was somehow able to know within myself that the choice before me was between short-term intense pleasure and long-term fulfilling marriage. I chose the latter and knew in my heart I'd made the right choice. Nevertheless, the experience left me giddy and amazed at myself.

I returned home feeling cocky, liberated and independent. It began to dawn on me that I didn't need Tony's work, Tony's friends, Tony's intelligence or Tony's inspiration to live an interesting and fulfilling life, or to do the things I wanted to do. I'd just spent two incredible weeks alone in Chicago and been happy the whole time.

My thoughts went immediately to the bike trip and I was convinced I wanted to make the trip alone, as Gerry had. Upon further reflection, however, I realized that a solo journey might be too much of a test for my new assertive self, and I searched for a happy medium. It became clear that this would be a women's trip. I wanted to prove to myself and others that a woman didn't need a man to take care of her in order to accomplish important things in life. I settled the fantasy in a secluded corner in my mind, resolving to remain alert for the opportunity I knew would present itself.

Eleven months later, at three o'clock on an afternoon late in March, I was snuggled on the kitchen couch reading the monthly *Bikecentennial News,* I always savored the articles and descriptions of summer trips, imagining myself on all of them. My eyes slid to the bottom of the page: "Cycling Companions Wanted," a section that reads like the "Personals" or the "Positions and Situations" sections of newspapers. I always enjoy fantasizing who the people might be in these ads, whether my life would be more exciting or easier with them than with Tony, or where I might go if I responded to one of them. My eyes scanned one of the ads, and my whole body instantly seized with a kind of excitement and anticipation I'd rarely felt before.

Woman, 29, looking for another woman to cycle across the country starting around May 1, 1978. Contact: Carol Golubock. San Francisco.

For a moment I wasn't sure that I hadn't put the ad in the paper myself; it all applied to me except the name. I saw the whole trip before me, even though I hadn't the vaguest idea of what "bicycling across the country" meant in practical terms. I saw the challenge, the adventure, the new people I would meet, the recognition and admiration, my chance for stardom. I saw the problems associated with leaving for two-and-a-half months. I didn't know if I could handle being away from Tony for that long. I would have to cancel our long-planned trip to Hawaii with our best friends, Tom and Paula. Plans for a million-dollar community project of which I was co-founder and director would have to be delayed at a crucial stage of development. I saw my sadness and anxiety at leaving my home, the plants and the animals in someone else's care. I saw the possibility of not getting along with this woman in the ad and hating the whole trip. I also wondered whether I could physically bike sixty or more miles a day when the farthest I'd ever gone was twenty miles in the flats surrounding our home town.

It took me thirty seconds to decide to call Carol. While the phone rang, I wondered what I would say. A secretary answered with the name of a place of business which I didn't make out at all. Carol came on the line and at once the fantasy became real.

"Hello?" It was a questioning, small voice.

"Hi. Carol? I saw your ad in the *Bikecentenniai News,* and I was interested in your plans. I've been thinking about the same thing for a long time."

She sounded surprised, as if she'd forgotten that she'd placed the ad. She told me briefly about her planned trip. As I listened, I tried to form an image of her. I was so nervous that I could do little more than catch the essence of what she was saying. She had already talked a few friends into joining her for parts of the trip. I wasn't sure I would fit in and became more nervous.

"Well, I'd really like to talk some more about it. Shall we get together?" I suggested hopefully.

"Yeah, that's probably a good idea."

I hoped it would be the next day; I didn't see how I could wait longer than that to find out whether or not I was going. I offered to come into the city for lunch and she suggested Thursday, two days away. We said goodbye and hung up.

She sounded nice on the phone, reminded me of myself—a bit shy, not too confident. I detected a subtle strength in her voice. I couldn't picture her though. I figured that if she were planning to undertake a feat such as biking across country, she was probably quite athletic, healthy, and full of energy. She'd be of medium to tall stature, physically strong. The fact that she was a legal aid attorney, which gave her a certain credibility and respectability, would be points in her favor when the trip came to be judged by my own attorney-husband.

As I biked to Walnut Creek to meet Tony for dinner at the local "Tia Maria," I was higher than a kite, excited beyond words and memory. Little Silver barely skimmed the road. I don't know how my skin was able to contain the force welling up inside me; I'd never felt such an intensity of emotion before: fear and excitement of the unknown, the fulfillment of a dream, the dread and eager anticipation of forming a new and intimate relationship with Carol, the challenge of the physical feat. As I sped down Danville Boulevard, I prayed that no squirrels or cars would dart in front of me to test my reflexes and cycling skills.

Of the thousand-and-one things bouncing around in my mind, the foremost problem was how to tell Tony about my wild scheme and win his support. Imagine announcing to your husband that in one month you are leaving with another woman for a two-and-a-half month cross-continent bicycle trip—particularly when he's a husband you've been stuck tight to like a fly to flypaper for nine years, *and* he's an attorney.

I figured my best strategy was not to *tell* him anything. My fear was that he would put me on the stand, so to speak, cross-examine me and then object. I would then become too frustrated and emotionally wrought to level a winning counter-argument. It was a scenario we had played out many times before. However, I argued with myself, since I honestly didn't know what his reactions would be, it wasn't fair to start out on the defensive. The best approach would be to share my excitement and the extraordinary opportunity I had to fulfill my dream. I was apprehensive, but also eager.

We met at the train station and loaded the bike into the car. I tried to listen attentively to his workday tales, but I was only half-there. I was waiting until just the right moment to announce my news. I held my secret until we were seated at a fountain-side table for two and had ordered our cheese enchiladas.

"Guess what?" I said, trying to balance my obvious exhilaration with a certain degree of reasonableness. "I have the opportunity to take a cross-country bicycle trip!!!!" He raised his eyebrows expectantly, so I proceeded. After a short, agitated description of events, I concluded with an unemotional, rational point to cap off my presentation. "And we're going to meet on Thursday to see if we like the looks of each other. Of course," I added wisely, "there are a lot of things to work out still, but I think it's worth pursuing."

So accustomed was I to being challenged with interrogatories, cross-examination and negative arguments—typical behavior for a good litigation attorney—that I scarcely believed my ears when he expressed tentative support for the idea. He suggested that I talk with other people who had taken similar trips, especially women, to find out the "true story" about biking in America. His concerns and my nagging fears were identical: Could the trip be made without severe consequences to body and soul? How many times would I be raped, beaten and molested?

I was ambivalent about talking to people. If America was too dangerous for two women cyclists, I didn't want to know about it. I didn't want my dreams smashed before I even left home. On the other hand, it would be impossible to look the truth in the eye and deny it. I certainly didn't want to be killed trying to reach my goal. Tony added how lonely he would be and that he'd feel a little rejected and abandoned, but that he knew how important this trip was to me, and he wanted to help me in any way he could.

I was astounded and touched. Ours had been a relationship based on a childlike dependence on each other and need for security. The prior two years had been marked by tears, tension and depression as I struggled, unknowingly, to gain my own adult identity, rather than the identity I'd accepted through Tony's work, his friends, his successes. My insecurity during this period of change had been reflected in my disdain for his work, habits and values, and my refusal to accept any advice or criticism from him. So I was surprised to be sincerely listening to what he had to say about my plans. He wasn't going to try to stop me; he wasn't going to try to make me feel guilty about leaving him. He was actually going to help me get this fantasy off the ground.

The night before I was to meet Carol I had a dream about her. It was a vision of two young women exactly alike. The identical twins were homely, with medium length brown hair held back in a hair band, their plumpish figures dressed in matronly plaid skirts and prim white blouses. The dream was puzzling.

At noon the next day, I entered the small corner restaurant and looked around expectantly. A very small young woman was standing in the corner behind the door. I almost passed by, when our eyes met—a questioning, searching glance—and I realized this was Carol. My heart sank. She couldn't have weighed more than 100 pounds and was several inches shorter than I. She looked no more able to bicycle across America than I did, and here I had been counting on this wisp of a woman to protect me from attackers! I hoped my disappointment wouldn't show as we picked up our vegetable quiches from the cafeteria line and sat down to discuss our future together.

While talking of routes and bikes, we each made a quick assessment of the other, of our own ability to fit in and get along with the other's personality. We were both feeling generally good about our first meeting by the time she had to get back to work, but decided not to make a final decision until we had spent a little more time together. We agreed to meet that Saturday for a bike ride and dinner at our house.

The weekend came and we set off for our ride. We couldn't tell anything about each other's biking because both of us were so nervous about whether or not our paces would match up that we weren't concentrating on biking at all. When we stopped at a fruit stand, I could see she wanted to tell me something. As we checked out with our under-ripe pippin apples, she said she'd forgotten to tell me one important thing—she was a vegetarian. She was greatly relieved to know that I was not a big meat and potatoes eater myself.

Tony liked her. He thought she seemed very sensible. In the late afternoon, the three of us sat out on our deck and looked over her maps and discussed the route she had planned. She had already spent a considerable amount of time thinking about how many miles a day to ride and what places to stop at. She had made vast lists and a preliminary itinerary. All at once, the reality of the adventure struck me full force. For the first time in four days, I began to feel scared. It finally dawned on me what I was about to do. Perhaps I'd been too hasty in expressing my enthusiasm. Perhaps this wasn't the right thing for me after all. Yet it seemed impossible to back out. I seemed to have already made the commitment.

Trepidations notwithstanding, we continued to make plans. By the end of the afternoon, we had agreed to leave on the first of May. It was then the first of April.

Preparations for the trip began immediately. I have never been absorbed in such a rainbow of unexpected and unknown feelings and experiences as in the month that preceded our actual departure. If I were, however, to choose one particular color that radiated most during that time it would be blue, and the corresponding emotion was an overwhelming sense of loss and separation.

I began to put my affairs in order so that I could be away for two-and-a-half months. With so many unknowns, I had little idea of what I was preparing for; being away from Tony for so long, being alone, riding a bike day after day for seventy-five days, meeting strange people, living closely with another woman, coping with new situations. Part of me wasn't sure I would make it back home.

I organized business for the restaurant project, which was in mid-design, so that plans could continue in my absence. I arranged administration of our home so that Tony could run the house, feed the animals, water the plants and pay the bills without undue hassle. When I told friends and other people I felt close to in the community about my trip, they reacted with disbelief, incredulity and enthusiasm. Most people thought it was an overwhelming idea, difficult physically and emotionally, but at the same time, it sounded like a very romantic adventure. I often saw in people's eyes visions of their own secret dreams, and the inner question, "Can dreams like this really be fulfilled?"

Telling Tom and Paula that we were cancelling out of the backpacking trip to Hawaii because of my trip pulled another carpet out from under my rapidly changing self-image. They were angry, hurt and disappointed. I alone was causing all this commotion and displeasure by following my own dreams and making my own plans. Hurting anyone, people or animals, was not an image I had of myself. I had gone to great lengths in my life to avoid causing people to be angry with me. But there was no way of avoiding it this time. I was so determined and convinced that this trip had a special importance to me that I was willing to accept the consequences.

The first member of my family to hear the news was my oldest brother in Santa Fe, New Mexico. I called Harvey to ask him about a route that would take us to visit his part of the country, through the high desert of Arizona and New Mexico. He minced no words in telling me the idea was very foolish, both the specific route plan and the trip itself. There were crazy and bad people in the country, he said, and I would be certain to run into some of them. I tried to explain that I was conscious of the risks I was taking, but that I thought I would be able to handle most situations. He described to me in gory detail the unpleasant experiences he and his wife had had while living in New Mexico, most of which I refused to listen to as I didn't need more fuel for my own vivid imagination. He did convince me, however, that we would be unwise to choose the desert route to New Mexico as it was little-populated and wild territory.

I asked him not to tell anybody else in the family so that I could do that personally, and I explained that I was going to Los Angeles that next weekend to tell my mother. He accused me of going in person just to see the shock on her face when I told her my plans. I was surprised and annoyed by his deep, psychoanalytic interpretation of my honorable motives. I hung up the phone feeling gloomy and hurt. The conversation hadn't gone the way I'd hoped. Harvey had always been my closest ally and brother when I was growing up at home. Instead of being supportive and enthusiastic about the trip, he was negative and discouraging. I began feeling more and more on my own, realizing my actions and decisions were totally mine. I would get no approval or support from those I'd always hoped to receive it from.

My mother's reaction was another surprise. I can't say she liked the idea, but she seemed to understand why I was going, something even I didn't fully understand. She and my stepfather Bill showed a great deal of interest in Carol and our proposed route. Bill told me how I'd smell the pine trees along the road to the Grand Canyon, as though he'd been there yesterday instead of thirty years ago. My relief and delight at her response was oddly mixed with disappointment at her lack of motherly concern. Wouldn't she worry about me? Didn't she care what happened to me?

Next I told Tory, something I was looking forward to because I knew my older sister would appreciate this kind of grand adventure. She was truly thrilled by the idea and excited for me. "Far out, Cookie Monster!" This was a childhood name I was becoming less and less fond of. I was feeling like I had outgrown the affectionate names we had for each other. I wanted our relationship to evolve to embrace who we were as adults and I thought hanging onto those old names would hinder that.

But still as "Cookie Monster" I showed her my maps and she bubbled with questions and exclamations and praise for my undertaking. But I was puzzled when she exclaimed, "You little rat!" and then, much to my surprise, she suggested that she go with me until we left California. My stomach clenched in a big knot. I had not intended to invite her, but at that moment I didn't have the courage to say no.

Wanting to postpone the inevitable moment of decision, we played around with the idea of her coming, talked about what she would have to do to get ready, what parts she would need for her bike. She was getting excited and part of me thought it would be fun too. That part of our relationship, as well as all that we shared in common, would be enjoyable on such a trip. On the other hand, I didn't want to deal with the competition we sometimes got into, and I didn't want to share the glory. Not this time. I wanted to go off on my own, make my own way, with no connections to my family.

My selfishness surprised me and I felt guilty for those unloving, unsisterly feelings. We decided to think about it overnight and talk about it again in the morning. I already knew what my answer would be.

When I told her on the phone next morning that it wouldn't work out, that I wanted to do this trip alone, she was hurt and upset. I wished I hadn't let the fantasy get started. I'd raised her hopes and she was understandably disappointed and a little angry. I felt guilty and miserable—but proud that I had been able to follow my strongest desires and stick to them. I said my goodbyes to family in Los Angeles and went back north to tell my older two brothers and my father.

At age twenty-nine, I was only slightly more than the Little Sister to Tom and John that I had been when we were children. Despite warm feelings between us, I was often impressed and intimidated by them, or felt put down by their patronizing or sexist attitudes. I wasn't at all looking forward to their questions or their analyzing my motivations for taking this trip. I wasn't so much worried about how my father would react. He was sixty-five, growing mellower by the year, and had always been an adventuresome sort of person himself. When we were little, it was always Dad who took us far out into the surf to duck the huge waves, or led us up the highest peaks in the mountains surrounding Los Angeles where we spent weekends at our family ranch. He happened to be visiting the Bay Area, so we gathered for a family dinner at John's house.

I waited on pins and needles for at least two hours before the right break in the conversation came for me to tell my news. My description of the trip came out in a kind of nonchalant, nervous excitement. They all looked a bit dumbstruck; Tom and John looked at Tony as if expecting him to acknowledge the little joke. When they realized I wasn't kidding, they asked me about Carol, the route, and how we would make the trip. The line of questioning made it obvious that they thought it was a crazy, risky thing to do. I was sure Tom and John were mentally listing all my subconscious motivations for taking the trip, but they were kind enough to spare me the details. Dad told me about the bicycle trip he and some college friends had taken through Europe; he clearly thought the idea intriguing and fun. We were chatting more about the trip when the phone rang. Dad's only sister, Aunt Caryll, had died after a long struggle with cancer.

At the funeral in Los Angeles, I said goodbye again to my family; this time to cousins, uncle, second-cousins, brothers, sister, mother, father and, of course, my aunt. Somehow, I felt my own parting similar to hers—a trip into the unknown that I knew I had to do. I was leaving all the security I had ever had in the real world behind: friends, family, familiar surroundings, home, my animals, my sense of belonging. Why was I choosing to leave all that? What was it that pulled me so strongly into this adventure?

My feelings about losing my old life and my loved ones persisted. Then, uncannily, I began losing material possessions as well. The first thing missing was an inexpensive gold ring that Tony had recently given me on our ninth anniversary. I'd worn it constantly for three months. Rings don't easily slip off fingers unnoticed, but mine did. There was not a trace or clue anywhere. Small things continued to slip away.

The next major loss followed soon after. I was biking into Berkeley—a kind of test run, using a map on unfamiliar roads. It was the longest ride I'd yet taken. I was going to meet a friend at the Buttercup Bakery for breakfast. On the way down a long winding grade into Berkeley, the bag which contained all my most important belongings—wallet, credit cards, watch—slipped silently off the back rack. I arrived at the meeting place several miles later to discover it gone.

I didn't panic at first, sure I could retrace my path and find it. Besides, by this time, I was becoming accustomed to this strange loss phenomenon. However, gradually I began to realize that it was just me and my bicycle in the middle of Berkeley with no money and no identification. I might just as well have been in Nebraska. I was totally on my own and would have to rely on other people to help me out of my predicament.

That was more than a little scary to me. I felt helpless and vulnerable. I'd never had to ask for money from anyone, nor had I been in a position where no one knew me to vouch for my respectability, responsibleness or financial position. I realized that was how it would be every day for two-and-a-half months all the way across the country. No one would know me, nor would they care who I was.

My friend arrived and we set off to find my bag, but with no success. I borrowed twenty dollars from an acquaintance—embarrassed and humiliated—and took the train home. I had to ask for a special temporary permit to take my bike on the train. The ticket agent was suspicious when I explained my regular permit had been lost, and he reluctantly issued a pass. I wanted to say, "Don't you know me? I'm Virginia Mudd and of course I have a bike permit!" And he'd say, "Oh yes, of course. Virginia Mudd. Yes, go right ahead." That was always the way it was growing up.

I was getting the message (by now delivered many times) to let things go, to free myself from emotional and physical attachments so that I could go on my journey with full attention and presence of mind. "When you get the message you can hang up the phone...."—wise words from a man who ran the local food store.

As philosophical as I was about losing things, I was totally unprepared and unwilling to accept the loss of one of our dogs. "Little Orphan Annie" had literally jumped into my arms while I was shopping in a busy section of Berkeley six months before. She was obviously one of thousands of Berkeley street dogs, and I'd had no success in locating a former owner. In a few days at home with us, she had wiggled her way into our hearts, mine being especially soft for lost puppies, and we adopted her. Annie had adapted well, but the older of our two Great Danes was left out of the two young dogs' play and began to express her jealousy by beating up on the younger Dane. It became obvious that the only solution to the problem was to give one of the dogs away, and it had to be Annie. Annie was the newest member of the family, she'd adapt happily wherever she went because there was nothing and nobody in life she wasn't enthusiastic about.

For several days I suffered the sorrow of having to lose her. It would have been easier if she'd gotten lost or killed. Just when I was resolved to take action, however, the dogs' relations seemed to improve. I held my breath. The Great Danes seemed to have achieved a certain degree of harmony, and by the time May 1st came, a week had gone by without incident. If peace continued, Annie would still be there when I returned.

The strangest part of the entire phenomenon of letting go was that everything I lost came back to me after I had succeeded in detaching from it emotionally. Tony found my ring in one of my new cycling gloves. When I'd tried the glove on, the ring had slipped off and stayed in the finger. Two weeks after I lost my bag, I received a card in the mail telling me that the Oakland Post Office was holding it for me. The money had been taken out and my pocket watch calculator had been run over, but everything else was intact. And, most important of all, Annie was still at home. I began to feel as if there were some magic about the trip, something that was helping me prepare myself, helping me put all the pieces together, so that the journey could begin. One other special incident reaffirmed this belief.

About a month before I had seen the ad in the paper, Gerry, the cross-country biker, now well-muscled and silently self-confident, had offered to help me give my bike a spring cleaning. He was working at a local bike shop at the time and had the use of the shop after hours. I was enthusiastic, yet I couldn't believe he really wanted to do that for me. So nothing happened. A short time later, however, he made the same proposal again and I began to believe that he meant what he said. We set aside one evening to accomplish the task; little did either of us realize what was involved in spring-cleaning Little Silver.

One worn part led to five others, each one grimier than the last, until the entire bike was stripped, cleaned, parts replaced and everything reassembled. Gerry was an ideal teacher and guide, unlike any I'd had before. He encouraged my most tentative and clumsy attempts at dismantling a mind-boggling assembly—like the crankset. He illustrated how to place the cone wrenches to tighten the bottom bracket, then how to listen to hear and feel if it were adjusted properly. He never took anything I was having trouble with away from me; instead, he explained what needed to be done, pointed out what signs to look for that would solve the problem, and only when I was completely frustrated and confused would he ask if I wanted help. I was a star pupil. In three sessions that lasted until 3:00 in the morning, I absorbed his knowledge, skill and tales of his own trip like a sponge, totally immersing myself in the study of bicycle maintenance. Little did we know at the time that this bike, Little Silver, was soon to travel 3,500 miles.

Of the two of us, Little Silver was in better shape by far than I was to make the trip. Emotionally, I was exhausted. Physically, I was overweight and out of shape even though I'd been biking ten to fifteen miles regularly. In trying to relieve my anxieties about the trip, I'd been stuffing myself with desserts, cheese and bread, a habit I'd picked up in the prior two years of great change and insecurity. My indulgence made me feel guilty, ashamed, out of control, and fat. I kept resolving to straighten out my act, but I was never able to muster the strength. All too soon, it was the first of May. The month of preparation was over.

Packing List—GEAR

Down sleeping bag
Foam ground pad
Space blanket
2-person tent
Extra tent stakes
Bike light (doubles as flashlight)
25-foot nylon cord
First Aid kit
Miscellaneous kit: duct tape, safety pins, needle & thread, rubber bands, Baggies

Mess kit: 2 aluminum plates, small pot, spoon, matches
Stove & gas canisters
3 water bottles (1 1/2 qt. capacity)
Notebook, colored pencils, pens, stamps
Form-fitting bike covers
Swiss Army knife

I'd not seen Carol at all during the month save for one afternoon we went shopping together for camping gear. On the phone, we arranged for her and her friend, Dave, to bike over from Berkeley to our house on Sunday, spend the night, and leave bright and early Monday morning. Dave was an old friend and biking companion of Carol's who taught at Stanford. He planned to bike with us until we crossed the Sierra.

Carol and Dave arrived in the afternoon. Dave immediately took off for a long hike while Carol and I stood around in the driveway looking at the bikes. Wanting to give everything important a name, I suggested "Big Blue" for Carol's Bertin bicycle. She gave me a quizzical look—as though it had never occurred to her to name a bike before—but the name stuck.

I had invited a few friends and family over for a farewell party that evening. My brother John, a doctor, was filled with medical advice for us; what to do for bee stings, diarrhea and heat stroke. Most everyone looked on in bewilderment as Carol and I sorted through piles of gear, organizing carefully and efficiently.

At 10:00 that night, Gerry arrived to say goodbye. For a farewell gift, he presented me with a small blue license plate that said "World Famous Biking Ace, Virginia," a good luck piece, and a small carved wooden box sealed with wax. I wasn't to open it until "things got really bad." Bewildered, I dutifully zipped it into a side pouch of my pack. By the time we went to bed, Carol and I were wound up as tight as clocks.

The morning was complete confusion. More friends came over to say goodbye, including the local press reporter and photographer. Annie had taken one of my cycling gloves and gone off to bury it. Carol was putting on clothes and taking them off, trying to get just the right combination. Dave was trying to feed everybody a good breakfast of scrambled eggs. I was alternately crying and giggling hysterically, while trying to pack my bike. Tony was crying and taking pictures of the great moment. I'd only seen him cry once—when Bobby Kennedy was shot—so I was deeply moved.

The moment of departure was even more poignant and dramatic. We held on to each other in several last embraces, not wanting to make the final separation. Carol, Dave and I lined up on our bikes at the top of our hill for press pictures. A few last goodbye hugs and parting words from amazed friends. "Have fun . . . take care . . . don't forget to write . . . don't forget me . . . I love you." Butterflies circling the knot in my stomach, tears streaming into my smile, I coasted off down the hill.

A half mile from home, we pulled over to make our first mechanical adjustment—3,499 1/2 miles to go.

Packing List—BIKE PARTS

3 extra tubes
Allen wrench
Tire irons
Gear and brake cable
Patch kit
Pliers
6" crescent wrench
Pump
Small screw driver
Chain tool
Free wheel remover
Extra spokes
HALT dog repellent
Spoke wrench
Gear Cluster: 14, 18, 22, 28, 34
Chain ring: 42, 52

Packing List—CLOTHES

3 T-shirts
2 pairs of biking shorts
1 pair *Beta* biking shoes
1 pair of tennis shoes
3 pairs of socks

1 pair of jeans
1 cotton turtleneck
1 wool sweater
Leg warmers
Fishnet underwear
Wool hat and gloves
Biking gloves
Hat
Gortex rain suit
Down vest
1 sweater jacket
Toilet kit: suntan lotion, tooth brush & paste, cream, lip balm, hairbrush, wash cloth
Sun glasses
Bathing suit

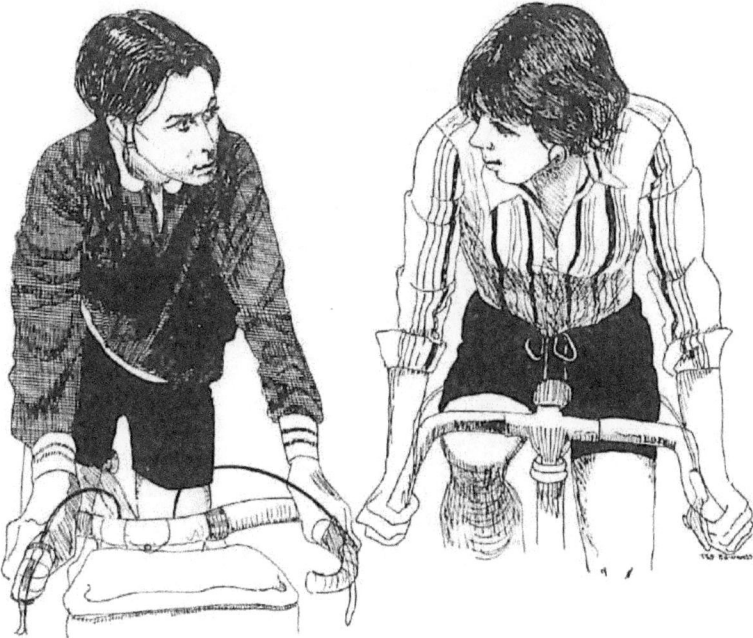

The Sierra

The sun shone bright and the birds sang sweet . . . . They were greatly pleased to see this delightful country before them.

DAY 1: Our first day on the road was a leap into the marvelous dream we had been imagining for years. It was wildly exciting, and scary. We were actually *Doing It*.

The anxiety beneath our excitement crept up on cat's paws—silent, slow, stealthy—and pounced ten miles from home. As we settled into a steady pace through the still-green countryside surrounding home, Dave asked us what our worst fears were about the trip. Carol had been in two serious biking accidents, so the dangers of biking were horrid and vivid for her. Her biggest fear was that she would be unable to complete the trip because of some physical problem. I, on the other hand, rode along in a state of innocence and naive faith that no car was going to hit me, no driver would open his car door and flatten me mid-stream, no gust from a passing truck would suck me into its grimy iron underside. My greatest fear was that Carol would tire of my company, or become fed up or angry with me, and leave. Of course, this drama would occur in the middle of the desert where I would be stranded without food, water or shade and no hope of a passing car for days. I hadn't acknowledged this fantasy before and was relieved to share it. In broad daylight, it began to look foolish and unlikely.

Most of that first day was divided between reveling in the astounding fact that we had started our cross-country trip, and coping with the practical realities of riding a bike loaded with thirty-five pounds of gear. The levee roads on the way to Stockton gave us our first taste of what it was like to share road space with 80-ton trucks. High gusty winds were blowing across the levee at the same time that the giant trucks passed us at sixty mph, creating turbulent vacuums in their wake. The winds caused Little Silver's front end to quiver uncontrollably. I expected the first breakdown with each shudder. We made it safely, albeit shakily, to Stockton, fifty miles away, and pulled into a Denny's for dinner. That first night, we slept peacefully under cherry trees in one of the many valley orchards, relieved and satisfied.

DAY 2: Shortly outside of Stockton, we began our ascent of the Sierra, a three-day climb that would rise through the agony of strained muscles, and the heartache of homesickness to a state of euphoria at an elevation of 8,500 feet. The day was hot and we treated ourselves to a deliciously cool skinny-dip in Commanche Reservoir, frolicking and giggling like children. When the local sheriff arrived to admonish us about our illegal swim, even he caught our excitement and pleasure and waved us on our way with good wishes for a safe trip.

The physical pain started shortly after our swim as we began climbing the steep, ungraded foothills which fan out along the base of the Sierra. By 5:30 I was near the limit of my physical stamina and good humor. Dave, however, was still going strong. He reminded me of a golden retriever; always enthusiastic and eager like a puppy, always full of energy, wiggling from head to tail with excitement. Dave's spirits seemed to rise with the elevation and his chatter kept pace with the rhythm of his pedals. He was oblivious to my subdued mood—growing fouler by the minute—and I began to wish for the first (but not the last) time that I were back home. What had I gotten myself into?

Homesickness settled in with a dull growing pain between my throat and left breast, while frustration and anger gnawed at my stomach. Afraid of what might pass through my mouth as a result of these unpleasant and unwelcome intruders, I pedaled ahead, trying to stifle sobs in order to get up the hills. I hadn't been able to make much progress, and Dave and Carol presently caught up with me. So did my tears. Sensing my overwhelming emotion, Dave pedaled on. Carol and I sat on the dry sagebrush bank alongside the road, and I reluctantly let the tears come. Here it was, only the second day, and I was already falling apart. What would Carol think? What would the future be like? She tentatively put a comforting arm around me. When I explained I was homesick, she said she had seen how close Tony and I were in just the few times she'd been with us and could understand how hard it must be for me to be leaving him. The more I cried, the less it hurt, and the longings for home and Tony subsided as twilight fell upon us. Having gotten over my first emotional mountain, we pushed on, caught up with Dave, and arrived in Jackson—Gold Country—by seven that evening.

One discovery we made over and over again on our trip, which always surprised and delighted us, was how eager people were to help us. So many times we were the beneficiaries of local folks' generosity and care. That evening we had the first of these surprises. We stopped after dark at a farmhouse on the outskirts of town to ask if we could pitch our tent in a nearby field. The owner studied us doubtfully. What a strange sight we must have been—two girls (Carol and I both looked more 19 than 29) and a middle-aged man wearing a bright orange crash helmet over a baseball cap, all wearing skin-tight black biking shorts, with three heavily-loaded ten-speeds. No doubt he was searching for a logical explanation for our presence on his doorstep.

He must have decided we were harmless enough, for after a few long seconds he offered us very elegant sleeping accommodations. At first we declined the use of his brand new luxury RV with two queen-sized beds which he had just brought home from the sales lot that day. It seemed too good for us to accept; he couldn't possibly mean it. To refuse, however, would have been to discount his genuine desire to be of service. With shy, appreciative expressions of thanks, we allowed ourselves to be led to our suite. Secretly we were overjoyed at such plush accommodations—no RV had ever looked so good.

I had an experience that night which I will remember as long as I live. Although my own challenge was not of the same magnitude, my effort to break through cultural and personal inhibitions reminded me of those survivors of a plane crash in the Andes Mountains who lived off the flesh of their companions who had succumbed to the elements. It took several months before they had the confidence and courage to publicly record their means of survival.

My survival had to do with being chronically constipated. I believed this was not so much a physical problem as an emotional state of being. Very young, I shut down on most of my spontaneous emotions for the sake of survival, for the sake of approval and acceptance by my parents, As I learned to hold in anger, hate, confusion, frustration, fear, love, joy, delight, I learned also to hold in my bowel movements, and later my menstrual periods, believing them to be ugly, unwanted aspects of myself. The condition wasn't helped by the daily inspection by household members to see what I had produced in the allotted toilet-sitting period. (Apparently, this supervision was the advice of the medical wizards of the day.) I had worried about what to do about this condition on the trip since I knew it would be intolerable to bike sixty miles a day with several days' worth of food in my gut.

As we settled into the camper on our second night out, I retired to the bushes to attempt a bowel movement. I was away so long that Carol called out to make sure I was all right. Why the hell couldn't I shit like a normal human being! Would I always have to spend thirty minutes of every day trying to rid myself of a few hard little turds of waste food? I began to panic, thinking about two-and-half-months on the road of this condition. In desperation, I cast my eyes about in the dark, searching for a spoon, a stick, something I might use to help the movement along. Nothing. Near tears, I realized there was only one thing I could do.

The worst of handling my own shit was in my mind. It was so ingrained that bodily smells, fluids and excrement are bad, disgusting, shameful and offensive that to be actually touching my own excrement in an attempt to get it out of my system was totally revolting and repulsive. Nevertheless, I continued the operation. After that first wave of revulsion, however, something surprising happened. I found the anatomy of my lower bowel to be fascinating. With a scientific detachment, I began to discover that I could sweep the little chamber clean. Along with the disgust, I felt a sense of power. I was taking care of a problem successfully and was no longer a victim of this predicament.

The experience had such a profound effect I was barely able to record it in my journal that night, and it was not until a month after we'd completed the trip that I could talk about it even to Carol. I had to repeat the process yet another time the next day, but this time I handled it more matter-of-factly. Day by day, movement became more free-flowing. I religiously drank a mixture of bran, flaxseed and water every morning until we reached the Grand Canyon. By then, the condition was so much improved that I let my body function on its own.

I fell into the queen-sized bed I shared that night with Carol, completely exhausted from the stress of emotions of our second day. What would the rest of the trip be like?

DAY 3: We pushed onward and upward the next day, and my body began complaining fiercely. I watched Carol and Dave churning out miles while I lagged behind with increasing pain in my legs and back and an incessant, unsatisfied thirst. No sooner would I refill my water jug from a roadside stream than I would empty it, still thirsty. For the first time in my life, I was scared of not having enough water to satisfy my thirst. Suddenly, the essential life-sustaining elements—food, water and sleep—became vitally important.

We were wonderfully compensated that night in a little mountain outpost called Ham Station at 5,000 feet. I could barely walk to our cabin when we arrived in the late afternoon, and gratefully sank into the tiny bathtub filled with hot steaming water. The bed was soft, springy and toasty, and I giggled with the pure pleasure of feeling it against my poor pained body before falling asleep.

DAY 4: The magic of the high mountains, the anticipation of reaching Carson Pass that day, lured us upward. We reached the snow line early in the morning. The glistening clean whiteness refreshed and invigorated me; it soothed my anxiety of wondering whether or not I could make it to the top. The air was pure and sharp, piercing my lungs as I sucked in deep breaths, one after another. Although we'd been expecting rain, the weather was still perfect, the sky a clear, deep blue; I felt we'd been blessed. Despite the cold temperature, we biked in shirt sleeves, only feeling cold when we stopped for lunch. We huddled inside the general store at Silver Lake, shivering and cramming peanut-butter-on-cracker sandwiches into our mouths.

By mid-afternoon, we cranked our last revolution to the crest of Carson Pass, 8,500 feet above sea level. We had crossed the Sierra on our own steam! The vistas of towering peaks and snow-covered mountains that we'd envisioned were sadly obliterated by high, dirty snow-machine embankments at the Pass—a small disappointment quickly forgotten in the glory of the moment. We took turns posing for photographs—arms across each other's shoulders—heroes and conquerors.

We flew off the other side of the Pass at eight times the speed we'd crawled up it. (If only it could have lasted eight times as long!) All previous downhill runs in my biking career paled in comparison to this one. What I remembered as steep, exciting hills became puny grades; what had once been unequalled speed was now a tortoise pace. While we managed somehow to keep our bodies connected to our bicycles, our spirits were irretrievably lost in space, speed and snow. I had never lived before. My usual inhibitions were hard put to conceal the extent of my elation and I shouted and whooped the whole way down.

The aching muscles, the glorious moments at the Pass, the flight through snow and time rose as warm memories, mingling with the steam and vapor from the baths at Grover Hot Springs where we relaxed in utter contentment in the early evening before pizza and bed in Number 6 of the Markleeville Hotel.

DAY 5: The day began with snow flurries. We left Markleeville bundled in our leg warmers, parkas and wool hats pulled low over our foreheads, headed for Monitor Pass (elevation 8,300 feet). Dave planned to leave us that day, but not until he had pedaled with us to the top of the Pass where we planned to have lunch. The climb was a tough one—we even had to walk occasionally. But what we'd missed in breathtaking vistas the day before was made up one hundred times over that day. I felt as though I were in a glorious dream, so hard was it to accept such beauty in the real world. I was oblivious to the pain, the straining lungs, the tedium of the long grind up the grade. Every eyeful was pure magic and fantasy. Was I Alice? Or Bilbo Baggins? Or Dorothy in the Land of Oz? Only the bitter cold and biting wind that cut through our layers of clothes like a knife through an angel food cake kept me anchored in reality.

When we arrived at Monitor Pass, we might have been in Siberia: the wind-swept, barren tundra, the leafless matchstick trees, the cold gray pavement slicing across an icy bowl. We searched unsuccessfully for a warm lunch spot and finally settled ourselves behind a small pile of rocks, determined to eat our peanut butter and crackers together before Dave left. But we hadn't realized how penetrating the cold was until Carol's fingers began to get numb; she became frightened. Dave and I worked over her hands, rubbed and patted her, then each other, but we couldn't generate a lasting warmth. We had to keep moving. Carol and I added another layer of clothes, our bright blue Gortex windbreaker tops and bottoms—our last extra clothes. We looked like two Blue Meanies. We hugged a hasty farewell and Dave turned back the way we had come, headed toward the warm, sunny Bay Area. We were so numbed by the cold that we had no time to react to the significance of his departure.

The extreme cold was a harsh intrusion into Wonderland. I was not the master of the Universe, the conqueror of the mountains I'd been just a day before. I was vulnerable and powerless before these forces. Anxious as we were to drop elevation quickly, we were forced to walk our bikes a mile down the mountain in order to maintain a few precious degrees of body heat. Then, deadly serious (now I know what that term means), we made our way quickly and carefully down the winding road on the eastern side of the Sierra, entrusting our lives to bicycle brakes.

At the bottom of the Pass, we stopped and snuggled between sagebrush against the barely-warm desert floor, trying to roast some of the chill out of our bodies. It was only then that we could begin to accept the reality of our situation; the cross-country bicycle trip by two women was officially starting. Even though Dave's enthusiasm had sometimes grated on my mood, he had been a good companion. It had been comforting to have him with us for those first few days—like having a man around the house. We hadn't had to deal with the anxiety of knowing we were responsible for our own fates, our own bicycles, our own way into the future.

We spent the night in a motel—with the heat on full blast—in Walker, California, on Route 395. Local folks told us it was unseasonably cold and we shuddered in agreement.

DAY 6: We awoke in good spirits and pedaled eagerly into the chilly, sunny morning, winding our way along a river as we began our ascent to Devil's Gate Summit. Carol shot out ahead and as the miles passed, I found myself growing increasingly anxious. My worst fear—her leaving me behind—began to swell in my body like a bee sting. When I finally caught up with her and confessed my fears, she assured me again she would never consider it, but I remained consumed by the nightmare. With great effort, I managed to hum a few lines from "The King and I."

Whenever I feel afraid, I hold my head erect, And whistle a happy tune, So no one will suspect I'm afraid . . . .

Much to my relief, the singing did drive the fear away, or at least back into the closet until another day. I resumed a contented pedaling up and over Devil's Gate.

The road to the next pass, Conway Summit, was again something of a challenge, and we stopped periodically to rest and take postcard photographs. Because neither of us knew anything about eastern California, we had no idea of the vision that awaited us. When we reached the top, our eyes beheld, below and beyond us, the vast, barren, Nevada wastelands, brown and deserted, stretching as far as we could see. In the foreground, the great inland sea, Mono Lake, lay like a jewel at the foot of the Sierra. Two hundred million years of geological history lay before us. We stood like two spellbound school children before the masterful architecture of the Sierra Nevada, understanding how the first human being to have seen this place must have felt. We decided to explore Mono Lake before stopping for the night in Lee Vining, and sped down the grade to its shores.

Mono Lake has a rich geologic and biologic history dating back over one million years. It is a salt water lake fed from the streams from the eastern slopes of the Sierra. In glacial times, the lake rose to many times its current level and overflowed into Owens and Death Valleys. Today, the water level is reaching dangerously low levels as the City of Los Angeles continues to divert incoming water from the mountain streams, raising serious environmental concerns. The lake's islands and waters provide the nesting habitat for seventy-five percent of the world's California gull population.

Tufa formations, the calcium deposits that emerge from the lake, give it a strange, unearthly quality and mystery. Carol and I stepped cautiously over the crusty, salted sand, moon-walking, sticking our fingers in the water to taste the brine, half-expecting to be sucked up at any moment by quicksand or lake monsters. Although we immensely enjoyed our exploration, we were relieved to leave the eerie shores of Mono Lake. After a big dinner in a Lee Vining cafe, we snuggled into our beds, fulfilled by summit climbs, discoveries, and apple pie a la mode.

DAY 7: Lee Vining is the home of "incredibly delicious," "not-to-be-missed" blueberry pancakes—or so we'd been told by well-traveled friends. So we scoured the town for this breakfast delicacy, our tongues turning blue with anticipation, but with no success. We settled for Lee Vining's version of French toast, a hefty piece of broiled white bread. After many cups of hot tea, we set off into the brisk clear morning, traveling south through the Owens Valley. Three miles before Bridgeport, we turned abruptly east and met face to face with an icy blasting headwind. I clenched my teeth with furious determination to withstand the unrelenting cold. Our bodies were still chilled by the day on Monitor Pass, and now we felt as if we had been returned to the freezer after only a brief thaw.

We huddled for lunch—jerry-tubed peanut butter and the last of our jam—in front of the Bridgeport courthouse. We explored the old town, visited the gas station and general store, and delayed as long as possible, knowing that biking twelve miles per hour would put us on ice again. Happily, after only a few miles, we turned south again along a mountain range and could use the same icy wind to propel us forward.

At this point in our trip, Carol was the chief map-reader and pathfinder; I was the carefree tag-along. Carol's previous biking expeditions had made her more adventurous in trying out side roads, while I was very content to follow the main highway, even if it meant gulping extra exhaust fumes. At least that way I was assured of not getting lost. Just before lunch, she led us off on our first excursion.

We left Route 395 north of Bishop. Reluctantly, I followed her down a long steep grade, knowing damn well there would be an equally long steep climb up. I tried to keep that depressing thought from marring the beauty of the back country; silver-gray sagebrush hills, rocky gorges, hardy pines thriving in a seemingly alien environment. I had to admit that the dramatic landscape was well-worth the bit of anxiety and extra energy. As we approached Bishop, irrigated plots of land were more frequent, willow and cottonwood trees flourished by creek sides, and tract houses dotted the hills. We stopped to watch a small herd of burros frolicking and grazing in a spring pasture. We guessed they were pack animals, which worked the warm-weather tourist season in the Sierra, now enjoying a few last weeks of idle roaming in their winter home. Indeed, even while we watched, two cowboys in a flatbed truck, outfitted with high rear and side railings, rumbled into the pasture, scattering the furry, feasting burros. Winter vacation was over.

Two Sunday cyclists rode up to us as we leaned against the fence watching the round-up. They were astride light pro bikes, dressed in hard core biking gear— black knit shorts, multi-colored pocketed jerseys and helmets. We envied them their uncluttered, sleek machines. The young woman was a student at the nearby University of California Geological Extension Center, and she invited us to stay the night there. We got directions and said we would arrive in due course. They sailed out of sight, leaving us and the burros to go about our cumbersome ways.

The Extension Center was a small green patch in the sage desert at the edge of Bishop. We took turns showering in the women's dorm, chatting with several of the students. Our hostess was eager to find out about our trip as she was obviously an avid biker herself. I secretly hoped our brief passage through her life would inspire her to take her own bicycle tour someday.

DAY 8: After seven days of glorious weather and trouble-free biking, Carol and I were both feeling as if we were due for a hard day. Nevertheless, it was an unwelcome change when it came. Having carefully studied the detailed maps at the Geologic Center, we left Bishop that morning destined for a side road outside of Big Pine that would keep us off the main highway for a few miles. I faked enthusiasm for this excursion.

We followed a winding paved side road through sagebrush country until it ended abruptly at the top of a small hill, far from the main highway. Glumly, we contemplated the gravel road that lay ahead of us, wondering how far it went. Not wanting to consider retracing our steps, we continued pedaling. We got more and more bogged down in rocks and pebbles and sand; I got more and more anxious. How would our bikes survive such rough treatment? When would the flat tire, the breakdown, come? I refused to admit that the gravel road was tougher than Little Silver and me as a team; I kept grinding on, putting everything I had into staying on that damn bike, shouting to myself and the bike, "Come on! Get your ass moving!" until deep sand gobbled up the front tire and we swerved into the ground.

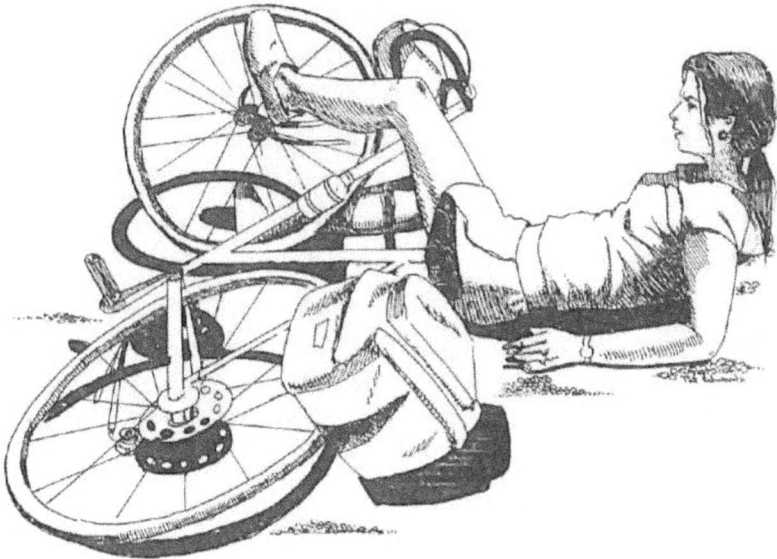

I was furious, hating everything—the road, the bike, the trip, Carol, myself. Carol was still fifty yards back; and I was glad that she hadn't seen my crash. Reduced to pushing my bike, I fumed and stalked ahead. I was startled from my fury by a dejected and resigned voice: "Hey, misery loves company." It took me a moment to understand that Carol wanted us to walk together. So foul was my mood I couldn't understand why she would want my company. She might just as easily have bedded down with a rattle snake out here in this God-forsaken desert. Besides, I had always lived my life along isolationist principles, doing everything alone. I wanted to be tough and brave and, above all, not to show weakness or need. But who was I to put those kinds of chains on her? So, side by side, the two of us pushed our bikes onward, in wretched humor, five miles to the main road. The highway felt like glass, and we vowed never, never again to risk taking a gravel road.

Despite our feeling that we'd paid our dues, another misfortune befell us as we left Independence in the late afternoon. Carol had a flat and, to add insult to injury, the replacement tube was the wrong size. Suddenly, we were broken down in the middle of California and no one was there to fix the tire for us! Carol was uncomprehending and frustrated; how had this happened? At first she blamed Oscar, her bicycle shop tutor; then she blamed herself for not checking the equipment more carefully. Anxious and embarrassed, we fumbled about for a quarter of an hour with an assortment of spare tubes and pumps, until an old pickup truck sputtered up next to us and the driver offered us a ride. Reluctant and humbled, we rode back to Independence—the only time we ever hitched or rode *back*—where we made some phone calls to Lone Pine, a larger town on our route south, to locate the right-sized tube. Our efforts were successful and we prepared ourselves to hitch the sixteen miles.

Our thumbs attracted an awesome tractor-trailer rig hauling eighty tons of—what else?—gravel. What had our thumbs done? What would Mother say? The trucker dismounted from the cab as Carol and I looked doubtfully at each other and then at the rig, trying to imagine how on earth we would get our bikes up into the trailer. While we pondered our situation helplessly, the great hulk of a driver came around the side, picked up first one bike and then the other and hoisted them over his head and into the truck bed. We watched in awe, then clambered into the cab alongside our well-muscled hero.

I thought I would burst with excitement. Ever since I'd watched "Cannonball" on TV as a kid, I'd had a fantasy of driving a big rig. Now, here I was. It was everything

I'd imagined: a shiny, maroon dashboard covered with little black and chrome dials and gauges; spiraling black cords connecting telephone, microphone, radios and stereos; a big, long stick-shift in the middle of the floor with switches and levers and wires—and *thirteen* speeds. Plus a bunk in the rear.

The driver couldn't get over what he'd picked up. Every now and then his eyes would leave the road for a brief moment and he would stare at us in amazement. He was curious and friendly, and gave us some useful information about the dynamics between bikes and trucks. He explained that it takes at least one-quarter mile to stop a heavy rig because of the tremendous momentum it builds up. If we ever heard a truck honk at us from behind, we should get our asses off the road, he said, because it probably wouldn't be honking for the hell of it. In fact, we found that during the trip, some truckers did honk just for the hell of it—to say "Hi," to honk encouragement, to make a snide or friendly gesture. But there were also times when they weren't kidding, and we were glad we had this trucker's advice to recall.

As we rolled along 395, he pointed out the site that had been the concentration-internment camp for the Japanese during World War II and told us a little history of the area. I was continually amazed by this man; he shattered all my concepts about truckers. Not only was he well-informed and interesting, but he had not laid so much as a finger on me even though my sexy, bare thighs (grimy from road grit in high-fashion black-knit shorts) were inches from his own. I was having so much fun that I was sorry it was such a short ride. He dropped us off in Lone Pine. As the rig roared into the twilight, I imagined his CB crackling into action: "You'll never *believe* what I just picked up." Ten-four, Good Buddy.

Mr. Gardner, of Gardner's Home and Sport Center, was just getting ready to close up shop and retire for the night when we arrived with Carol's wheel. As arranged, Mr. Gardner had the right size tube all ready for us; but we discovered a new set of problems—we didn't have the right size tube and valve combination to fit her wheel. Carol had three choices: get a whole new wheel; have new tubes sent from home, which would take at least a week; or enlarge the hole in her rim so the available valve/tube would fit through. Unperturbed and relaxed, Mr. Gardner analyzed the problem. I stood by feeling very helpless, hoping this man could solve our problem, hating to be in such a dependent position. I breathed a sigh of relief and thanks when Mr. Gardner said he would be happy to stay late at work and drill a bigger hole for us. He amazed me because, in my experience, people would rather sell a new product than help preserve and repair the old one. That he ran his business under these preservation principles, and that he was willing to spend time and energy after business hours to work on our problem, made him a very special person.

The hole was drilled, a new tube tested for fit and minor adjustments made. By 7:00 p.m. we were on the road again—straight to a motel room for a bottle of wine and a bath—feeling very fortunate and grateful.

The Desert

At the East, not far from here, there is a great desert and none could live to cross it.

Day 9: By the time we left Lone Pine, Carol and I had begun to feel more secure and confident about our trip. We knew by then we could get along with each other; we'd crossed the Sierra; we'd managed to successfully come through the gravel road and flat tire episode on our own; our bodies were in good shape and I was no

longer homesick. Once across the Sierra, we'd been able to bike between fifty and sixty miles a day—right on schedule. All of this changed, however, in the unbelievably difficult passage through 220 miles of desert.

My only experience in the desert had been from within air-conditioned hotel rooms or automobiles, where the only time sun hit flesh was during the hurried trip from the car to gas station restroom and back. Now, as we turned east from Lone Pine in bright sun, in nothing but short-sleeved T-shirts and shorts, I sensed that I'd never really been in a desert before.

Our first stop at 10:00 a.m. reinforced my growing uneasiness. Keeler was a "town" eleven miles from Lone Pine: we had looked forward to a cool drink in the shade there before tackling the midday heat. We were dismayed and a little shocked by what we saw. From where we sat under a scruffy willow tree, everything we could see—house trailers, old wood shacks, an occasional parked car, shrubs, trees—was covered with a layer of fine, dusty sand. Just looking around made me thirsty. The gas station was dilapidated and boarded up; we could find no water spigot anywhere. Fortunately we'd purchased an extra quart container for water at Mr. Gardner's and filled it, otherwise we would have been in trouble.

The only sound came from a light wind blowing gently through our willow tree, stirring up small whirling dust storms on the sandy roads. Then silence. Where were all the people? There wasn't even a dog to bark at us to let us know we weren't the only ones alive in this ghostly place.

There was not a cloud in the sky; the sun was hot and bright yellow. A strong, constant headwind met us as we left Keeler, fanning billows of hot air into our faces. It was like being inside a clothes dryer. There was no shade; just vast expanses of dry, barren land with a sixteen-foot-wide strip of bright, black asphalt slithering across it. The landscape was so exposed, so whipped bare by the force of the wind, that little grew upon it. No lush growth, no frills; just a few stark, sparse grasses and brush.

Several miles from Keeler I noticed that I was pedaling furiously, breathing excessively fast, despite the fact that the road was relatively flat. My heart was racing. My whole being was deeply frightened, and I pedaled faster to out-distance a terror that had no form. With the sun and wind and heat beating relentlessly on me, I began to feel as naked as the desert, exposed and stripped of false laughter, quick light-hearted replies, pretty faces, tailored outfits from I. Magnin, and manners suitable for Buckingham Palace. Stripped down to the bones and blood. It was as if brutal, violent, faceless people had grabbed me, thrown me against a wall, torn all my clothes off, and forced me to run naked through the streets of downtown Los Angeles. Words began to form in my mind—the beginnings of the first poem of my life, the only response I had to this terror.

Composing the poem as I pedaled diverted my emotions from the agony of my nakedness, and I began to reflect on how I had come to such a hellish place in my life. I knew when I left on the trip I would have many memorable and dramatic experiences. I was even looking forward to those unknown challenges, but this was much more than I had bargained for. Was this my reward for two years of struggling to come to grips with my life?

As the mountains were exhilarating so the desert is demoralizing

The wind whips and blasts at the sand castle I have spent twenty-nine years building

The drawbridge has caved in, the guards have deserted, the wind prowls the corridors of my soul

In the main hall the wind dines on a banquet of fears, hurls goblets of aloneness crashing to the floor

The fear of death gnaws at my bones, howls up the stone cold staircase I have laid with blocks of icy smiles, constipation hard as rock

—vm 5-9-78

At the age of twenty-seven, I "discovered" I had problems. I was shocked— an image of myself exploded. Heretofore, I'd considered myself a well-adjusted, unharried, relaxed individual, not plagued by the petty problems that bothered other people. I saw myself as a perfect wife, mother (to my animals and plants), community and political activist, conservationist and homesteader. I was a model for Right Livelihood, a specimen of good health, and had perfect eating habits besides. I never touched or so much as laid a lustful eye on white sugar or flour products, and I was a strict vegetarian. I was running several cross-country miles a day and had weighed 102 pounds for a year-and-a-half. Having been overweight all my life, I was delighted by the New Me. My friends and family were concerned about my low weight but no one said anything about it to me, and I was totally satisfied with the new look. But something was wrong; something was happening. I was twenty-seven, married eight years, and, aside from losing forty pounds, hadn't changed a lick in all that time.

The rumblings and volcanoes bursting within me erupted in the form of compulsive eating. At first, I thought nothing of my desire to consume a half pound of cheese in one sitting. After all, I could afford to eat a little extra. I remember well the first time I noticed I was eating to satisfy some hunger other than physical. It was February 15, 1976. Tony and I were having breakfast at my mother's house in Los Angeles, where we had spent a few days visiting. It was exactly one month before we were to give a big fund-raising dinner at our house to benefit the California Nuclear Initiative. It had been my idea and I'd coordinated the whole affair. I was very excited and nervous about it. Dr. John Gofman was coming to speak, and I hoped to have at least thirty people, all contributing $30 each.

When I ate more scrambled eggs than I wanted that morning, I attributed this odd behavior to pre-party excitement. But I started becoming "excited" all the time. Soon I couldn't pass the refrigerator without opening it and finding something to put in my mouth. At first I restricted myself to "good" food—whole wheat bread, cheese, nuts, natural food sweets, honey ice cream—but as the months went by, I found that that wasn't enough to satisfy my insatiable craving to have food in my mouth, to taste good flavors, to swallow. I expanded my food repertoire to include just about anything I could sink my teeth into: whole loaves of zucchini bread (sometimes straight from the freezer), double scoops of ice cream, bags of corn chips. Frantic. Panicked. I would consume food all day long. Then I would eagerly await dinnertime when I could cram my face legitimately with more food. The guilt and embarrassment that followed these binges were devastating. I would lie on the kitchen couch with my stomach so bloated it looked as if I were pregnant.

Unconsciously I'd tell myself what a dreadful person I was, how I had no discipline, will-power or self-control whatsoever. I'd never been so out of control before in my life, and it scared the shit out of me. I couldn't understand what was wrong with me—why I couldn't stop eating like a raving maniac. What made matters even worse was that at that time I was cooking for children and teachers at the preschool I had co-founded, so I was constantly around food, I had every opportunity to indulge my lack of self-control—and did. I was supposed to be a nutritionist for the school; I'd set up the food and snack program using only natural foods, no sugar, no preservatives, etc., etc. What a joke. Some nutritionist who is secretly a food junkie!

I didn't tell anybody. Every new morning, I'd vow that today it was going to be different; something had changed overnight—in a dream, in a vision—and I'd be back to normal. It never happened. I was gaining weight by leaps and pounds; I had reached an alarming 112 pounds in a few weeks. I was scared to death that I would become fat, and I decided that the only remedy was to fast. I'd fasted previously for short periods of time (two or three days), but now it had to be something more drastic. I billed it as a super-cleansing health treatment, a very high spiritual event, and I fasted for ten days on two separate occasions during that year. I thought surely— hoped desperately—that would break me of the habit I was now firmly locked into. It didn't. And as if to make up for the food I'd missed during the fast, the security I'd denied myself, I'd get over the fast and consume ever-greater amounts so that I had soon surpassed the weight I had been at the start of the fast.

It was crazy, insane. I was beside myself. Occasionally I'd mention to Tony that I couldn't understand why I was eating so much (no big deal, you know). He'd reply that there were times when he'd eat compulsively, too; it was nothing to get so upset about. I didn't even know what it was like to feel hungry anymore. I couldn't bear to have an empty feeling in my stomach; everything else in me was feeling so empty as it was.

I knew something was going on, something bigger than either of us could understand. And one day, in early 1977, as I was biking home from Walnut Creek, I became conscious of feeling physically, emotionally and mentally numb. I was so burdened by the quantities of food in me that I really couldn't tell if I were me or not. Was I still there? I was devoid of even an ounce of energy; I don't know how I was able to pedal because I felt nothing. Nothing. I was a zombie.

I decided that I had to do something. I resolved that perhaps I had been too thin, and that my body was trying to tell me that it needed more of a certain nutrient. Surely that would explain the frantic consumption of all food. I was 123 pounds by the end of the year, but actually during the course of the year—feasting and fasting and frantically bicycling off a few calories—I'd probably gained closer to fifty pounds. My fear of being fat was all-consuming; it was the only thing I thought about in my waking hours. If I were fat, Tony would leave me, men wouldn't look at me, women would ignore me, everyone would cast scornful glances at me, and I'd be out in the cold. It was an unbelievable nightmare.

In search of the missing nutrient, I made an appointment at the Wholistic Health and Nutrition Center in Mill Valley for a complete health exam. It included a nutritional analysis, blood and urine tests, an iridology exam, a palmist's reading, a spiritual interpretation, and a stress evaluation. The iridologist, palmist and spiritual guide all had approximately the same vague observation: that I seemed to be unbalanced in some way, taking in a lot of energy with no place to put it out. I didn't understand what they meant and was baffled and disappointed. The stress evaluator asked me about my marriage. What, I wondered, did that have to do with anything. Of course, it was fine. Any other questions?

At my final consultation, I admitted that another reason I was there was because I had not had a period in more than a year since I'd stopped taking birth control pills. The doctor suggested that I see someone in Berkeley by the name of Linne Gravestock. I assumed she was a gynecologist or some other M.D. specialist. It wasn't until I arrived innocently at her house for my appointment that I realized she was a therapist.

Reluctantly I began a year-and-a-half of therapy. I had no idea what was before me. It took several months before I learned the difference between *saying* I was upset, or angry, or miserable, and *being* all those emotions. Even more than crying, I hated to raise my voice in anger. "Don't raise your voice, dear," my mother's words resounded in my mind. The only weak spot in my intellectual defense lay in my dreams, which were filled with truths about who I was and how I was feeling. With Linne guiding me, holding my hand, I relived nightmares of tidal waves, bludgeoned whales, murky, slimy pools and chase scenes. Slowly, painfully, I began to discover what I was hiding under mounds of butterscotch marble sundaes, zucchini bread and fudge pie.

During the worst of it, I was afraid I'd never make it through therapy alive. In the best of those months, I was depressed, floating through life like a piece of protoplasm. I spent a good deal of time crying. One evening Tony came home from work to find me dissolved in tears, huddled by the speaker of the stereo which was blaring at full volume. He wondered out loud if I was really "getting better." While I struggled for myself and often against him (we were rarely able to communicate our feelings to each other), he secretly feared that after my tears and rage, I would leave him. Indeed, as my emotional barriers crumbled, I was simultaneously building my own strength and independence.

In such a vulnerable, delicate period of change, I began the bicycle journey, knowing, dreading, that I would uncover a great deal about myself during this two-and-a-half month, twenty-four-hour-a-day therapy session. Once I'd opened the gates on the parts of me that I'd kept locked in for so many years, it was next to impossible to shut them and I wasn't sure I wanted to either.

That first morning in the desert, I was so physically beaten down and emotionally battered that I thought I was going to die. I'm not sure I would have been able to slam the door in Death's face and on my emotions even if I'd wanted to. All I could do was to keep pedaling. In those miles of hell, I recalled the time I was fifteen and volunteered at the Children's Rehabilitation Center in L.A. One patient was a boy who had been so badly burned that he had little hope of living more than a year or two. His body was covered by a thin purplish layer of raw skin; his voice was a rasping guttural croak. He was hideous to look at. I knew now how he must have felt.

At some point, when I could go no further down, my perspective began to change. I began to see a little beauty in the desert; the pastel colors, the delicate artistry of a sage leaf, the crags of the rocks, the tiny organisms growing on their bare faces. As if I saw through the looking glass of my fairy godmother, everything became magical and serene, and I felt myself, in all my nakedness, becoming peaceful—even beautiful—even willing to die in the desert, for I felt its beauty would bring peace to my soul. For the rest of the day, I rode in a state of tranquility, admiring and loving everything around me.

Towards evening, we descended on a winding, wild-flowered road into the Panamint Valley, a long, flat, narrow land lying at the western edge of the mountains that surround Death Valley. Our goal for the night was Panamint Springs, which we imagined to be a tourist town with a motel, gas station, souvenir shop with postcards, and a cafe, maybe even a grocery store—all the amenities we longed for. We thought— hoped—we'd taken a wrong turn when we saw that our "oasis" was a dust-covered clump of willow trees and an abandoned hotel where only scorpions and sidewinders lived in dark corners. As we pulled up at the front door, we saw that there were two other equally-disconsolate and disappointed bike tourists there. As we sat on the porch sharing our miserable fate, a military jet—speeding, flying bullet-machine—flashed no more than 100 yards above the valley floor in front of us. Awesome. Frightening. We learned later that the Panamint Valley is a military testing area.

The hotel must have been beautiful at one time, perched as it was on a hill overlooking purple and pink dawns and flaming sunrises, its front lawn shaded by a venerable, graceful willow tree. Now, it was ominous, threatening and disappointing. Nevertheless, I went to explore the ruins, eager as Tom Sawyer. The guest rooms had been stripped and all that was left in the main lodge were a few overturned tables and chairs. Carol was spooked by the place all the while we were there. She tried in vain to persuade me to put my sleeping bag on the porch with hers instead of under the willow tree and stars. It was comforting to know there were four of us in that lonely place. We ate supper and visited with our two biking companions, who were on their way to Arizona from Northern California. We didn't particularly enjoy their company, especially when they turned on their radio after we had all gotten into our sleeping bags. When they finally turned it off, we fell into uneasy sleep, listening for ghost noises and the padded steps of tarantulas.

DAY 10: We were still there at dawn. I awakened before first light softened the darkness and woke Carol. We ate a small, dry granola breakfast, and before our fellow travelers were up, we set off across the valley floor, hoping the jets were not testing at 5:00 a.m. In the cool, silent dawn, we traveled five magical miles in half-light toward the mountains, and the gateway to Death Valley.

We climbed steeply up 3,500 feet for over three hours—one of the hardest climbs of the trip for me. The grades were steep and by the time we were two-thirds of the way, the pain in my knees was sharp and steady, and I worried how much damage I was doing by persevering to the top. But I forgot all about it when we reached the summit at 10:00 a.m. and reveled in the glory and pride of conquering yet another mountain. Vacationers in RV's and loaded station wagons passed us with looks of wonderment on their faces. Expecting the usual glorious and swift descent, I was more than a little irked to discover a rutted, rock-strewn and narrow road on the other side of the summit. We bounced and braked—I grumbled—down a full 5,000 feet to sea level and below, to the lowest elevation in the United States—282 feet below sea level. We arrived in a half hour at Stove Pipe Wells where we had a can of fruit juice and a rest in the shade. It was amazing how little we needed or wanted to eat. After some indecision, we decided to attempt to reach Furnace Creek and the Visitors Center before the sun beat us off the road.

It was an excruciating twenty-four mile ride. The temperature was over 100 degrees and the wind was unrelenting. The landscape of cracked salt flats and white glaring sand offered no relief. We were crossing the floor of an ancient lake, formed by melt-water flowing from the Sierra Nevada glaciers during the Ice Age. Due to the arid conditions of the region, the lake had eventually receded; vegetation grew sparsely and soil accumulated slowly. The exposed rock formations had become a favorite site for prospectors in the Gold Rush days of the early 1900's. Visions of the 20-Mule-Team Borax trains—the clanking and shifting of the harnesses, the shouts of the borax miners, the choking dust of twenty sweating mules— rose through the heat haze to meet us. This was *Death* Valley.

We didn't stop for twenty-one miles. We took turns breaking wind for each other. When we slowed down, the heat was too intense; we had to keep moving so the wind could cool the sweat on our bodies. Within three miles of Furnace Creek, we collapsed in a small grove of willow trees (the first trees we had seen), as near to exhaustion as we were ever to be on the trip. Neither of us had realized how brutal the conditions were in the desert and how cautious we had to be to survive. We sat under those few little trees, quiet and serious, lucky to have found that shelter.

Three long miles later we arrived, with no energy to spare, at Furnace Creek. In a daze, we followed directions to the pool, dug out our bathing suits from our packs, changed, and slipped into the ice water bath. Nothing had ever felt so good; our whole bodies were orgasmic as we floated and dived, splashed and sunk into the cool blue depths. We revived quickly. We moved from the pool to the air-conditioned restaurant and spent the hottest part of the day luxuriating in the icy air and the first "real" food of our day.

Eventually, we ventured over to the Visitors Center where we watched a film and studied displays of Death Valley. We began to gain a small measure of appreciation for its geology and natural beauty, something we couldn't see before. When the Center closed to the public at 5:30, we lingered, hoping that no one would object to our spending the rest of the evening and night on the lawn. When all seemed quiet, we unloaded our gear and spread our picnic on the lush green grass: sardines in mustard sauce, tomatoes, Seasoned Rye-Krisp, Lancer's Rosé Wine, and ice cream for dessert. The struggles of the day fading but not forgotten, we relaxed completely, thoroughly enjoying our luxurious accommodations so far away from the reality of the desert just a few hundred yards away. We dropped into our sleeping bags shortly before dark, and slept happily and peacefully all night.

DAY 11: The struggle with the sun and wind continued the next day. As usual, I awoke before light and waited patiently until it was reasonable to ask Carol to get up too. We set off as dawn began to bathe the valley in cool colors. We savored the beauty of the early morning desert, knowing it would soon be obliterated by the midday sun.

By lunch time, we'd climbed out of Death Valley and arrived at Death Valley Junction, a peculiar sort of ghost town whose half dozen or so inhabitants apparently refused to believe their town was no longer a thriving tourist spot. Many years before, a flood had left the town in ruins, and since most visitors preferred the more luxurious modern conveniences in Furnace Creek, it was rare that any traveler wanted to spend time in the town. We heard this brief history from the caretaker/manager of the hotel which stood in one corner of the square. In spite of the fact that no one ever spent the night, the dilapidated hotel was immaculately maintained on the inside. The lobby was decorated with large, healthy plants and the ladies' room wore a fresh coat of bright orange paint. It was as if guests were expected at any moment.

As we turned south, headed for Shoshone, we were met by another dreaded headwind, only this one the strongest so far. I became more and more frustrated because I knew I could be traveling at least fifteen miles per hour on this flat smooth desert road, but in the face of the oncoming wind, I could only go half that speed. My only consolation was knowing that for any bicyclist a persistent headwind is far more discouraging and humiliating than the steepest hill. After fifteen miles of fighting the wind in 90° heat, my emotions boiled over. I screamed and cursed and cried, barely conscious of my legs still cranking the pedals. Why is it so hard? You can't do this to me! Don't you know who I am?

At the heart of the pain burned the realization that the wind could care less who I was, that all the money and privilege in the world wouldn't make a bit of difference in making it any easier to bicycle through the desert. I wasn't accustomed to struggling for anything, to working hard for a goal. I'd always had immediate solutions to problems in the material world: plumbers always came immediately to fix the overflowing John, a broken toy was promptly replaced by a new one. Now, not only couldn't I pay someone to remove the wind, but I couldn't even call home for someone to pick me up. My wealth and class were of no value at all.

I didn't believe we would ever reach Shoshone. On top of feeling emotionally terrible, my knees, already strained from the push to Towne Pass, were hurting severely. I was close to tears again as we finally reached the outskirts of town. We found a public pool where I was able to relieve the aching in my knees under a flowing water spout. As if they sensed my troubles, people in Shoshone were especially kind to us. At the local bar, two men, Vince and Jack, bought us wine and listened with interest to tales of our adventure. Perhaps I was naive to believe their intentions were completely honorable, but I enjoyed and needed their attention and interest. That night we slept in a grove of pine trees near the local elementary school. The gurgle of the creek and the peace of the evening were like a cool smooth salve on a raw wound. The pain and trials of the day began to slip away.

DAY 12: The very next day, as if in a magical gesture of balance, we received a treat that we remembered for the length of our entire trip and will for the rest of our lives. We turned north from Shoshone, determined to bike the twenty-six miles to Pahrump, Nevada, before having breakfast. I resigned myself to the headwind that again greeted us, and the miles passed slowly, but not unpleasantly.

Six miles from Pahrump—just after crossing our first state border—we came upon St. Nicholas himself. He was a grand old gentleman, lively and quick, with a twinkle in his eye and a well-trimmed white beard, and he was driving a team of six gray, long-eared donkeys hitched to a buckboard. A newly-born, all-white, baby donkey trotted freely along beside. It was a sight to lift the darkest spirit. Despite our hunger, we couldn't pass up this wonderful scene, so we stopped a hundred yards ahead and waited for the team to catch up. "St. Nicholas's" name was Herman Morgart. He and his donkeys were the main tourist attraction in town, he said, and he took many children for rides on his buckboard. When we told him we were looking for breakfast, he directed us to the Cotton Pickin' Cafe. When we said goodbye, with promises to send him copies of the picture we'd taken, I felt that if nothing else good happened on the whole trip, this one sight would have made it all worthwhile. To top off our morning, the Cotton Pickin' Cafe also gave us the best breakfast of our entire trip: Spanish omelets and the best homemade baking powder biscuits I have ever tasted. We dubbed them "Pahrump Biscuits." All across the country we searched for other "Pahrump Biscuits," but they only exist in one place.

It was at times like that, eating a delicious and satisfying meal that we came to appreciate the significance of food in our lives. Eating had become one of the most important activities of our day. What we ate had to nourish both body and spirit, and we spent considerable amounts of energy visualizing, planning and selecting our meals. Fortunately, Carol and I had few disagreements about what or how much to put into our stomachs.

We were "natural food" fans. Neither of us cared for red meat, we stayed away most of the time from white sugar and "junk food," and compulsively read the labels on packaged products. We both loved raw fruit and vegetables and agreed that we didn't want to cook a lot on the trip. Breakfasts usually consisted of granola (until halfway across the country when we refused to eat another spoonful), dried fruit and sunflower seeds. In our second month, June, we'd buy a melon the night before and have that with plain yogurt about once a week as a special treat. We rarely ate breakfast out, but when we did, I delighted in being able to put down a full order of pancakes and eggs, knowing I wouldn't gain a pound.

Our taste for lunch went in cycles, the featured foods being cheese, peanut butter or sardines; we'd overdose on one before switching to another. Bread sat like lead in our stomachs so we never ate any after one or two sandwiches early in the trip. Instead, Seasoned Rye-Krisp, discovered in Death Valley, became our Wonderbread—baked to a perfect crunchiness after hours in the hot sun on the back of Big Blue. We'd almost always top off lunch with an apple and some other fruit. We switched to bananas in Kansas when a lady in a health food store told us to be sure we got enough potassium.

Dinners were by far the most enjoyable meal of the day. At breakfast, we were usually apprehensive about the unknowns of the day and anxious to find out. Although we were somewhat more relaxed at lunchtime, it was just a short break in a day full of visual, physical and emotional stimulation. We only indulged ourselves in complete relaxation at dinner time. At last, the biking day would be over, no more hills to climb, no headwinds to face, no trucks to fear, no potholes to dodge, no decisions to make. We could unwind with total abandon.

Upon our arrival at the last major town of the day, we'd find the most likely looking grocery store and make a careful inspection of the whole place before making our selection—usually fresh vegetables for our special salad. Sometimes it was no more than a soft carrot, withered head of purple cabbage, and a rubbery anemic tomato. Other times it was a magnificent assortment of crookneck and zucchini squash, fresh mushrooms, ripe, succulent avocados, crisp green peppers and cucumbers, and a golden ear of corn. Then we'd pick a suitable dressing—yogurt and lemon juice and hot mustard was the favorite—and select a couple of other items, such as cheese or tuna fish or beans to accompany the main dish of salad. Dessert was usually dried fruit.

About every third night we had wine—not every night so we wouldn't take it too much for granted, so that it would remain a special treat at the end of the day, our reward. Buying a bottle of wine always put us in a festive mood and recalled good times back home. It warmed and soothed our tired bodies and sometimes anxious minds. After a few cups, we'd fall into our beds, deep into sleep.

Dinnertime was special for us in other ways, too. Chopping vegetables was meditative and restful, and provided an interlude between high-energy biking and calm evening activities. Once our meal was prepared, we'd sit on the ground (or on the floor in a motel room) facing each other, mess plates in our laps, and reflect on the day's events: the sights, people, road conditions, our own feelings, our own developing relationship. Whatever physical or emotional hardships we endured during the day faded into a warm haze of satisfaction and contentment: a hard climb would transform into a warm glow of accomplishment; a painful knee or crotch would dissolve with the wine into a dull hint of an ache. We sighed a great deal at that time of the day—sighs of relief, of pride in our accomplishment, of acceptance of our new surroundings and the anticipation of a good night's rest.

We left Pahrump and the Cotton Pickin' Cafe feeling fully compensated for the agonizing desert miles we'd biked to get there. I felt relaxed and self-satisfied, relieved that the worst of the desert was over, happy with myself for getting through it. My personal pleasure was heightened by my anticipation of meeting Tony the next day at Lake Mead.

I had been talking with him every day on the phone since leaving. It was a way to reassure him that I was all right, and a way for me to share each day's adventures and accomplishments with someone back home. Carol and I had decided that we needed to take a day or two off our bikes and that this would be a good time for Tony and me to see each other. He joked about needing to see that I was actually biking across America and not in sunny Acapulco with some Latin Romeo . . . . My mind was completely preoccupied with our reunion. Would I recognize him? Would we be able to talk to each other? Had I changed? Had he? Would we have sex? How would the three of us get along? We were eighty miles away from Boulder Beach where we had planned to rendezvous mid-afternoon of the following day. Our maps indicated that our next thirty miles would be on a needle-straight road across heat-scorched desert. The prospect of being roasted like a juicy piece of chicken for two-and-a-half hours was even less attractive on this Friday afternoon when people would be whooping their way to Las Vegas for a night on the town. So contrary to our usual style, we decided to ride side by side and talk to each other to help pass the miles. We knew we would hear an approaching vehicle in time to slip apart in single file.

The only sounds to break the heat and the silence of the lonely desert were our voices and the whir of our pedals. We were deeply absorbed in our conversation of my reunion with Tony when suddenly the silence was shattered by screeching brakes and skidding tires. A silver-gray pickup truck swerved wildly around us into the opposite lane and sped away down the road. We were scarcely able to believe what our eyes and ears told us. How had we not heard that truck? How close had it come to hitting us? Shaken, we continued on carefully, with a vague sense that we were being guided and protected by some "Divine Spirit." An hour later we arrived at Mountain Springs, a small settlement on the top of the hills surrounding the Las Vegas area. As hot, exhausted and unnerved as we were, we were doubly grateful for the local bar that was open for business. We drank several glasses of ice water before ordering wine spritzers.

As we were describing our adventures to the bartender and the juke box service man, the bar began to fill up with other travelers. The wine was doing its work and I was feeling relaxed and happy. I was unusually out-going and confident, eager to talk with the people at the bar. I was surprised and angry when Carol pulled me outside and said she thought I was being indiscriminate about whom I was talking to and that we should decide what we were going to do for the night instead of spending a lot of time socializing. I felt censured. Maybe I had been too open, too expansive with strange men. Was I secretly looking for some guy to come onto me?

I stopped wondering about it all in order to make a decision about what to do for the night. Rather than risk going into Las Vegas at dusk, we decided to camp on the summit in the shelter of the pine grove across the road. Hidden by scrub pine, we ate our last supplies of tuna fish and crackers and retired.

DAY 13: After a beautiful early morning downhill into the Las Vegas area, and a quick detour onto an interstate, we biked the rest of the remaining twenty miles to Lake Mead with some of the most unpleasant, obnoxious, aggressive and loud motorists that we were ever to have the misfortune of sharing the road with. Unfortunately, it was a Saturday and the campers and power boats were out in force. It was obviously a cheap thrill for some of the younger drivers to see how close they could come to hitting us without actually touching. A car full of beer-drinking teenagers would flash by within inches of us and a loud cheer would erupt from the car. Hot vacationers eager to get to the water honked and tailed us if they were unable to pass on a tight curve. We arrived at Lake Mead in foul humor; my joy at my imminent meeting with Tony completely destroyed. Plunging into the lake cooled our rage, and we stayed until the skin on our fingers began to shrivel. We'd just finished sprucing up in the public coin-op showers and were settling down at the main entrance with some cold "V-8" juice when Tony arrived.

He stopped the car where he found us, and we were in each other's arms as he opened the door, giggling and staring at each other giddy and drunk on our reunion. Eventually, we managed to come down to earth and piled all our gear and ourselves into Tony's tiny rent-a-car for the drive to Boulder City five miles away. I had to *laugh* at us, jammed like sardines into that sporty white Mustang. One long-standing difference Tony and I have is over the kind of car we like to rent when we travel. I like mini-cars, Hondas or Toyotas, because I feel more in control. Tony likes big cars so he can put as much steel and plastic as possible in between himself and the perils of the road. This time, however, he had made a special effort to rent the smallest car available. There we were, the three of us squished into two bucket seats, with the wheels of the bikes hanging out the Mustang's tailgate. We couldn't even use the air-conditioning.

As Tony drove us around Boulder City to the Laundromat and the health food store, I was reminded of the few special occasions when Mother and Dad would drive to boarding school for a weekend and take me out to dinner and into the big city of West Hartford to do a little shopping. In both cases there was an indescribable sense of relief and pleasure in being able to turn myself over to people who proceeded to do wonderful things for me. We spent the afternoon watching a movie about Hoover Dam (in an air-conditioned theatre) and, afterward, lying peacefully on the lush green grass of the Boulder City park. Filled with a Mexican dinner, we set out to locate a campsite.

We had decided on a place called Willow Beach because it was on our route south. As we drove to the Colorado River, at the bottom of a four-mile grade, we felt like loaves of baking bread in an oven; the farther we descended, the hotter it became. The campsites were trailer-size asphalt spaces surrounded by clumps of flowering oleander bushes. Campers and station wagons piled high with gear and screaming kids wound their way slowly through the aisles looking for a vacant slot. It had all the charm of a parking lot in the Sahara Desert. With a twinge of guilt at our weakness, we retreated, deciding to find a motel at Lake Mead. The room we found had two double beds and an air-conditioner of sorts. What bliss. Tony and I tucked into one bed and Carol into the other. We all felt a little shy and uncomfortable at first, but the heat of the day and our tiredness soon relaxed us to sleep.

DAY 14: While the morning was still cool, Carol and I sat out on the veranda in front of our motel room and cleaned our bikes. It was disorienting not to be on the road for the first time in two weeks, and to have Tony there made our situation all the more dreamlike. We moved through the day in a happy daze. We escaped the midday heat by descending into the bowels of the earth beneath Hoover Dam. I was awed and a little frightened by the huge rumbling turbines over 500 feet underground. Despite the contempt I felt for man's manipulation of Nature in this way, I was impressed by the magnitude of the project: the thousands of people who had worked on it, dumping one bucketful of concrete after another, for days, weeks, months, years, on end. They must have had the patience of Job. And yet, how easily it could all be flushed down the river if Nature suddenly took a violent turn. A quake would collapse the concrete masterpiece into a pile of rock, dirt, mud and raging water. We humans play with our blocks, while Nature builds the Grand Canyon and the Tetons.

On leaving the dam—crossing into Arizona—we appreciated Tony's visit for yet another reason. The intense, concentrated heat had turned the asphalt road into a smear of hot, sticky tar and oil. Cars passing over it sounded as if they were driving on rain-slick pavement. The thought of riding our bikes across it made us groan with relief as we motored along.

Since Willow Beach put us in a good position for an early departure in the morning, we again descended into the furnace by the river, this time with reservations for a motel room there. As the day ended, we sat by the river and cooked our "Sesame Burgers" and sipped wine The three of us had spent the whole time together, enjoying a weekend of exploring, relaxing, and easy conversation. The time had been too short and not private enough for Tony and me to reestablish any kind of intimacy, and it was just as well we didn't try because we would surely have been disappointed and frustrated with our inevitable failure. Sex was out of the question; but I had little interest or desire for it anyway. Perhaps it was having a bicycle seat crammed in my crotch seven hours a day that had numbed my sexual appetite. It was one thing I never missed the whole trip.

As the evening wore on, the sadder I became, thinking of the little time left for Tony and me to be together. We slept in each other's arms through the night, enjoying the warmth and closeness that would soon be over.

DAY 15: Next morning we were back on desert working hours again. At 5:30 a.m. Carol and I posed for photographs beneath the road sign: Kingman—our way—South; Las Vegas—Tony's way—North. We fiddled and delayed as long as we could; I felt like a piece of Velcro being torn apart from Tony. I fought back tears and sadness, longing to go home with him. As we got on our bikes, Tony, through his tears, said to Carol, "Take good care of her."

As we turned south and headed straight into the unmerciful headwind, the memory of his love did little to lessen the pain I felt. I wondered if the reunion had even been worth it. Carol and I had established a good routine and my homesickness had vanished—until now. On top of the ache in my heart, my crotch hurt for the first time, and my knees were still painfully sensitive. I wished over and over that I could be at home. By far the hardest single lesson I had to learn—over and over during the journey—was how to be exactly where I was. I would want to be at home, or in the next town, or in a motel, or finished with the whole trip. That inability to live each moment for itself made me miserable on many occasions—heading toward Kingman was one of the most wretched and frustrating of all. Because of the headwind, I wasn't moving *anywhere* at even a *reasonable* rate of speed. I was really hooked on speed, on getting places quickly with the least amount of unexpected delays. Now, with every crank I fought the wind. I wasn't progressing, wasn't moving ahead. Carol stopped to wait for me. I pulled alongside of her and apologized for being silly and childish. Here I was, falling apart *again!*

The tears washed away some of the pain, but the heartache was still there as I settled my protesting crotch onto the seat again and slipped into Carol's wind stream. As grateful as I was for her strength and comfort at times like these, it bothered me that she didn't have any troubles of her own. I didn't like feeling as if I were the only one with problems. I never knew how she was feeling—not until much later—and it made me so uncomfortable. She's my mirror, I thought. She keeps her feelings and problems (if she has any) to herself.

With the exception of those times, our relationship was an easy one. We were so committed to the trip that we were extremely careful to avoid conflict and to be sensitive to each other's feelings. Not that there would have been great discord if we hadn't been so cautious. We got along very well. Our moods were similar, we liked the same foods, liked the same biking routine. We both preferred the solitary experience of biking, riding just within visual distance of each other. Both of us had a high tolerance for physical discomfort and rarely complained. We talked very little during the day, and at night our conversations were usually quite serious.

Not until our trip was nearly over and I had developed some perspective did I realize just how serious we both were. In sixty days, I don't remember either of us ever truly laughing with abandon, ever totally giving ourselves over to gay frivolity. Only once, in Colorado, when I was provoked by extreme circumstances, did I let myself go. Our subdued mood, however, was not without its lighter moments such as that very same awful morning when we came upon a tiny Arizona outpost called "Santa Claus." The doll-size grocery store, now abandoned, that marked the town of Santa Claus was flanked by two giant red-and-white striped candy canes. It was such an absurd, bizarre sight in the Middle of Nowhere that I momentarily forgot Tony winging his way home and cheerfully ate lunch, wondering when Santa Claus had last been here.

We made the mistake of asking about the incessant headwinds at the agricultural inspection station outside Kingman. To our great dismay, we were told that the winds would be with us for another sixty miles. What good did it do us to find *that* out? We bought some excellent vegetables at the Kingman Safeway and, after patrolling the small city, decided on the city park for the night. The wind blew and tugged at the postcards we were writing and flapped our journal pages as we dutifully recorded our day.

As we snuggled into our sleeping bags, we realized that we were camped directly underneath a street light—the first of many in other campsites that we discovered after dark. But sleep overcame us before we had a chance to become seriously annoyed.

DAY 16: I absolutely hated the morning. Headwinds, homesickness, and those fucking trucks barreling down Route 66. I screamed and cursed. How could I gracefully get out of this damn trip, I wondered. I thought about calling Tony and

asking him to concoct an emergency so I would have to go home. I thought about just telling Carol straight out that I hated it all and didn't want any more of it. But how could I admit defeat like that? Impossible. What else? I could get hit by one of those trucks, just enough to make bike riding impossible. When I saw myself lying underneath one of those monsters, however, I decided I'd gone far enough with my escape fantasies. I imagined myself slowing down, checking the traffic behind me, then pulling out into the middle of the road, crossing the double line and heading west, back to the Kingman Airport. I pictured that several times just to see how it would feel. It didn't feel good at all. Something stronger and deeper than my present mood kept me riding east, following Carol.

At that moment of knowing I would not turn back, I suddenly realized I was pedaling up a grade in *high* gear! My God, a tailwind! I held my breath so it wouldn't go away, savoring every inch of highway as it flew by. What a thrill! We sailed through Valentine, Peach Springs, and Grand Canyon Caverns. Within six hours, we blew into Seligman, Arizona. Eighty-three miles in one day!

DAY 17: I woke up the next morning nervous and feeling cold for the first time in a week. I poked my head outside to discover a hard-blowing crosswind. Oh shit! I looked longingly at the RV's parked in the KOA campground with us, so massive and bourgeois, so warm and comfortable. I was becoming rather bored with my attitude about headwinds and tried to think why I was so hung up about them; why so nervous, so afraid? It occurred to me that my anxiety might be arising from a basic and deep belief about myself of "I can't." Did I hate the wind so much because I was afraid I wouldn't be able to cope with it, wouldn't be able to make my way through it? The wind put up such a mighty force which I constantly pushed and heaved against, only to come upon it again and again. With the realizations that I thought I *couldn't* and that I shouldn't have to work so hard to attain my goal, I felt I'd uncovered the major source of my trouble. Maybe it would explain other anxieties. Meanwhile, with the headwind howling in Seligman, I repeated to myself, like "The Little Engine Who Could," *I think I can, I think I can, I think I can—I know I can, I know I can...."*

On top of my new-found discovery and growing self-confidence, blackberry pie a la mode at the local cafe in Ash Fork, twenty-five miles east, was almost too much good stuff to handle in one morning. It's hard to imagine what wonderful little places there are along back country roads. This cafe was small, homey and full of warm kitchen smells. It was owned and managed by two older women who took an instant liking to us and talked with us while we savored our chili omelets and blackberry pie.

The scrub brush, sage and grasses of the high desert plateau changed rapidly outside Ash Fork to rocky pine forest. Back in the mountains again with the fresh pine smells, crystal clear air and brilliant blue skies! This, plus the absence of the Route 66 trucks, made my spirits soar. We arrived in Williams, twenty miles away, in the early afternoon and stopped at the Safeway for dinner supplies. There, parked in front of the store, were the bikes belonging to the two with the blaring radio we'd passed the night with in Panamint Springs. We were eager to ask them how they had fared in Death Valley. It turned out that we had been wise to start off that morning as early as we did. They had barely made it to Stove Pipe Wells and, because of the heat, had had to stop there for the day. When we learned they had been hitchhiking, Carol and I inwardly patted ourselves on the back, knowing that we had cycled that distance.

We left Williams after sitting awhile in the sun and writing postcards. We wanted to get as close as we could to the Grand Canyon so we could arrive there the next day in plenty of time to sight-see. We wound our way north toward the Canyon through pine forests and cool evening air. The wind still blew, but I felt strong and confident, so high on the mountain air and my own personal victory over the wind that I scarcely noticed it.

Even my first flat tire of the trip (after 800 miles) didn't dampen my spirits or arouse any anxiety. In fact, the scene was almost comical. We'd pulled off the road into the pines and set up camp close to the railroad track. Just as we settled down to enjoy our salad, Little Silver let out a great "poof," and the front end instantly collapsed. I gasped in surprise and then burst into laughter. Nothing could have ruined my day at that point.

DAY 18

The Grand Canyon of Colorado . . . as unearthly in color and grandeur and quantity of the architecture as if you had found it after death on some other star . . . .

—John Muir

Chills ran up my spine. I felt out of time, out of this world, insignificant, yet one with the Universe as Carol and I sat on the rim of the Canyon—me for the first time—absorbing it, absorbed in it. The colors changed constantly in the late afternoon sun. I thought we must be in the most beautiful spot on earth—and to realize we had arrived there by bicycle from California! We had pedaled over the Sierra and across the Western Desert to this magnificent vision. Every time I had said to myself, "I can't," I had pedaled another seventy miles and proved that I could. I *was* doing it. There was progress every day—no getting around it, no way to maintain the helpless attitude that made it easy for me not to try. This sense of independence and personal accomplishment was almost as awesome to me as the Canyon itself.

We had a wonderful celebration that evening. We "dressed up" in our fanciest clothes: cotton turtlenecks, blue jeans with green thread stitching, Adidas instead of Beta biking shoes, and pullover sweaters. With our bronze faces and ruby red noses layered with peeling skin, we felt very glamorous entering the lodge for our dinner reservation. We dined on Rock Cornish game hen and fish, cheesecake, a California wine and an after-dinner liqueur. In that relaxed, almost romantic, atmosphere, we talked openly and honestly about ourselves, sharing secrets and intimate thoughts of our families, sex, relationships with men, expectations and fears of the trip. I confessed how close I'd come to turning back outside Kingman; she admitted she'd had her own doubts about whether or not I would actually come the whole way with her. I realized that for me the Canyon was a goal fulfilled and that I now looked forward to the days ahead, instead of back to California.

As we walked back to our room, I only wished we could have held hands. The delicious, candle-lit dinner, a subtle, warm alcohol high, the moonlit magical Canyon, made me want to reach out to her, to tell her how much I cared about her. But how would she interpret that? Would she think I was a lesbian? Was I? I'd certainly had plenty of fantasies of loving women, and rather liked the idea. Loving Carol, loving me—was there a difference? But I didn't want to scare her, didn't want anything to get in the way of our making the trip together. We walked on side by side.

DAY 19: The route leaving the Canyon was glorious—if only it could have lasted forever. To the south was the Kaibab Forest with its miniature, rich-smelling pines; to the north, the Grand Canyon stretched for twenty miles, a mirage of vivid colors. Cobalt-blue desert sky, timeless rock and canyon walls—it was so idyllic, so perfect. How fortunate I was! We stopped at the last scenic outpost with a view of the Colorado River far below, a thin muddy stream in the depths of the Canyon. Tourists lavished us with admiring stares and questions. We collected their attention like treasures, using it as fuel to help us on our way.

Sailing down a long glassy highway, we left the Canyon for good. The smaller canyons that carved out the mesa on our left made me feel as though I were witnessing the formation of another Grand Canyon. In our descent of over 2,000 feet, we came into new territory; new geological formations, new vegetation and ecology, new terrain and new people. We entered the Indian lands of Northern Arizona.

Just outside of Cameron we were stopped by a highway patrolman who warned us that "the Indians would just as soon hit ya as look at ya." I tried to ignore his and my prejudice as trucks full of young Indians on their way to Tuba City for the night blasted their horns at us. No painted ponies here; only metallic painted pickup trucks with western country scenes painted on the rear windows in day-glo colors.

Seven miles from Cameron, fifteen from Tuba City, we had our first mechanical breakdown. Carol's rear derailleur refused to shift into low gears; it was impossible for her to climb hills. We carried on, walking our bikes on up-grades. Actually, we feared for our self-images as much as anything else. It was easy to forget our embarrassment, though, as we biked through the Red Desert, through some of the most glorious, delicate scenes imaginable. Soft pastels blended into richer shades of pinks, rust and red. The moon, like a puff of cotton, rose slowly, slowly in the baby-blue evening sky. I imagined I was on Mars.

I awoke from my dream upon arriving in Tuba City, in the middle of Indian country, at nightfall. There was just enough light to see that there wasn't a tree in sight, let alone a city park to camp in. We felt stranded—Palefaces in Redman's territory. We sought refuge in the local 7-11 (oh, thank heaven for 7-11), taking some comfort from the familiar fluorescent lighting and bright plastic packages. We found ourselves surrounded by a slowly circulating crowd of Navajo and Hopi people. What I would have given for a foolproof disappearing act! No one was openly or even subtly hostile toward us, yet I felt their eyes penetrate to the core of my being. Their faces reflected nothing; the black glowing eyes revealed no signs. They seemed to regard us without judgment, coolly, and go on about their business, reserved and closed to us.

Even without the disappearing act, I felt invisible. We weren't "stars" here. No one made a fuss over us. Recognition as a reward for a hard day's biking was out in Indian country. I realized how much I depended on and desired other people's recognition of me to determine my own sense of worth; how much I needed other people to like and admire me. Carol and I, the intruders, would have to form our own cheering section, congratulate ourselves, feel good about and like ourselves, all by ourselves.

The owner of the 7-11 store, an Anglo, offered his backyard to us for the night. We gratefully accepted his invitation, relieved to take our bikes and ourselves out of sight. On a tiny patch of grass under a scrawny tree, we fell asleep to the drone of the store's air-conditioning unit.

DAY 20: There were anxious moments in the morning while we studied Carol's malfunctioning derailleur. Fixing it was as much a psychological problem as it was a mechanical one. Having been raised to be an inept, helpless female, I was intimidated by mechanical things and frightened of their failure, convinced I'd be unable to fix them. Commonplace flat tires—a routine repair—caused me considerable anxiety. I would struggle against my self-doubt, question my competency, even after successfully changing scores of them. Carol's hunch that the derailleur spring had broken had been right. Fortunately, Oscar had given Carol two spare springs to take with her, thereby redeeming himself for neglecting to put in the right-sized tire tube which Carol had needed earlier in the journey. We found the right tools and moral support at the local auto parts store. The mechanic on duty was a large, clumsy, gentle fellow who was eager to help. I wasn't sure he understood the dynamics of bicycle repair, but his eagerness to help and kindness went a long way toward solving the problem. Soon we were on the road again.

The shapes and forms of our new world on the fringe of Monument Valley were dramatic and grand. Rocks, mesas, even the clouds, were more majestic than we'd ever seen, almost like sculpture. The Old West came to life—stagecoaches rumbled across the desert, posses galloped in hot pursuit of a black-hatted bank robber, war-painted Indians on spotted ponies lined the crests of the mesas, poised for ambush.

The farther we rode into Indian country, the more we began to understand their distrust and suspicions. The Indians worked in the mines, the stores, the trading posts, but they didn't own them. They added cultural flavor and authenticity to the businesses—the right touch for tourists—but the white traders and entrepreneurs, who were the owners, received the benefits. And this on the Indians' own land. As we pedaled past Black Mesa, it became apparent that the environment and land were held in approximately the same low esteem as the people. The Peabody Coal Mining Co. was hard at work, stripping.

And the coal company came with the world's largest shovel
And they tortured the timber and stripped all the land.

Well, they dug for their coal 'til the land was forsaken
Then they wrote it all down as the progress of man.

John Prine's song ran through my mind and I hummed the mournful tune as we passed the Black Mesa—an ode to the lost land, innocent, beautiful and helpless.

"And, daddy, won't you take me back to Muhlenberg County
Down by the Green River where Paradise lay?"
"Well, I'm sorry, my son, but you're too late in asking
Mister Peabodys coal train has hauled it away."

That afternoon, we gave a small cheer as we passed the 1,000-mile point of our journey. Seemingly just to test our ability to overcome obstacles, Carol's rear gear cable broke. While we were well-prepared enough to have along an extra cable, we had not been so clever as to include in our tool kit a good pair of wire cutters. Consequently, cutting the end off the new cable left it as frayed as a witch's broom. How were we ever going to thread it through the tiny hole that connected it to the shift lever—before those black threatening clouds dumped rain all over us? For twenty minutes I held the cable with one pair of tweezers and Carol painstakingly twisted the wires with the blunt wire cutters into a tight coil. I wasn't at all convinced we would succeed in the task and more than once had to restrain myself from throwing my hands up in helpless dismay. But knowing there was no other choice, we persisted. We felt very proud of ourselves when the job was completed and the cable installed.

In Kayenta, for lack of any natural shelter whatsoever, we spent the night in the small, local motel. Dinner pickings were slim, but the postcard selection was more than adequate to keep us busy well into the evening.

Postcard and journal writing had become an important ritual for both of us. Over the course of the trip, I sent over 120 postcards. I kept a careful record of who got a card on what date so the news could be spread around. We usually wrote cards three or four times a week, depending on the supply of picturesque cards (In Kansas, much to our surprise, there were none to be found.) We had one rule about postcards: you couldn't send it unless you'd seen it or been in the area. We felt it would bring bad luck to send a postcard of a place we hadn't gotten to yet. After biking off one state map and onto the next, I would send the used map with a letter to Tory, indicating the places we had camped.

The last thing we did every evening before going to sleep was to write in our journals. There were five sections to each of my entries: places, distance, terrain, weather and highlights. In the last section I collected all that had affected me most deeply during the day. Emotions I hadn't wanted to express could be written down and punctuated with exclamation points or little drawings. By the time I had spent twenty minutes writing I was satisfied that the important moments were saved and the day could end officially. There were several occasions, however, when the nighttime was more eventful than the day, which always threw my well-organized system into confusion.

DAY 21: We had expected nothing so beautiful as the stark and spectacular country we were in, and we cycled along in delight. We continued our passage through this high country desert region where even the names—Moenkopi, Canyon de Chelly, Mexican Water, Teec Nos Pos—were enchanted. Every panorama was filled with magnificent shapes and rainbow colors in crystal-clear air. We were particularly captivated by the Red Mesa, a perfectly shaped mound of reds, purples and magenta seated on a creamy lime-green grass plain, looking for all the world like a boysenberry cheesecake.

By 5:00, we reached the Four Corners Monument where we posed for our picture with our feet firmly planted in four states. We crossed into Colorado to look for a camping place by the San Juan River. We were hesitant since we would be trespassing on Indian land. Finally, we resolved that we would probably be forgiven our trespass under the circumstances, and carefully and laboriously lugged our bikes and gear down the embankment. We tucked ourselves into a clump of bushes at the bottom of the slope and began our evening routine.

The Rockies

They could see the road of yellow brick running through a beautiful country, with green meadows dotted with bright flowers . . . .

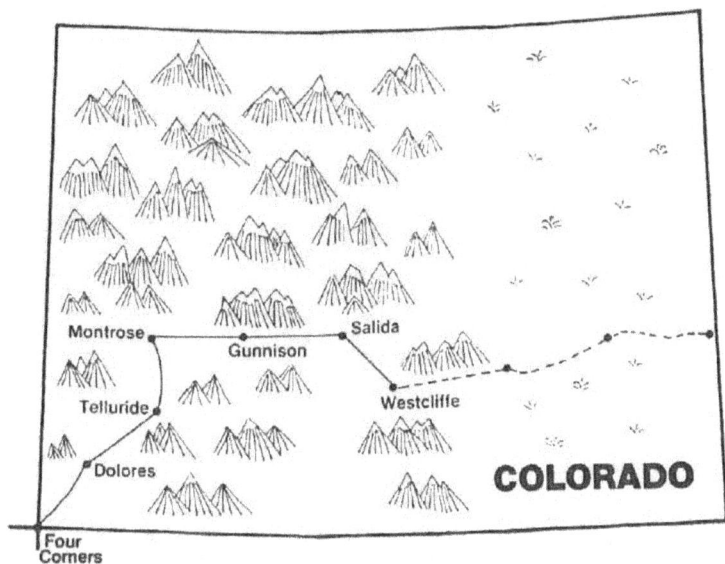

DAY 22: Biking in a northeasterly direction into Colorado, once again the environment began to change around us. It always surprised me that even in the short space of a day's ride—between fifty and eighty miles—the ecology and topography would change so noticeably. Of course, there were stretches of days where the earth's dramas unfolded only slightly, as in Kansas or Northern Arizona. But even in those states, we always saw subtle transformations in the land: a different species of pine, a few more succulents, a slight rolling of the terrain, a little less humidity. In other

areas, the scenery changed like a slide show, suddenly and miraculously, a whole new environment in a day's journey. It was at these times, when we entered a new world, that we had to spend some time acclimating to our new surroundings and developing a new routine that fit the weather, terrain, ecology and inhabitants, including humans. Moving from Northern Arizona into Colorado was such a time.

We traveled on a road that climbed like steps up to Ute Mountain. I was relieved to be leaving the Indian reservations and refreshed by the sudden appearance of running water which gurgled and splashed by the roadside. Soon we were surrounded by lush pasture land, crisscrossed by streams, laced by borders of aspen and evergreens. Far off on the horizon were snow-capped mountains. The Rockies at last!

We saw them for the first time at 12:30 p.m.—the great wall of Colorado. "But how are you going to get over the Rockies?" The question most asked by our friends back home echoed in our minds. We had wondered the same thing ourselves, but didn't want to think about it until we had to. They were as alluring as they were formidable. Like a magnet, I was drawn to those barely-visible snow-capped peaks, as yet scarcely distinguishable from the cumulus clouds above them.

Our anticipation and excitement grew exponentially. When we arrived in Cortez an hour later, we began to prepare ourselves for the assault. First, we started the washing machines rolling at the Laundromat. Naked under our Gortex shells, we sat down to write a few Colorado postcards while we waited. Our second stop was the "All You Can Eat for $2" buffeteria—our first. We were as shocked as they were at the quantity of food we put away. We consumed samples of everything they had to offer, leaving in our wake piles of finger-licked plates.

During this food orgy, once again good fortune came to us in an unexpected way. Blowing his cigarette smoke across our spread of dishes, a diner at the next table altered our route. We had planned to follow the so-called Million Dollar Highway through the Rockies. The road was the pride of the auto industry—a million-dollar engineering feat—and heavily traveled by tourists. Our "guide" suggested we take a parallel road, Route 145, that he assured us was equally scenic and less busy. But this would mean passing up a trip to Mesa Verde. Neither of us knew anything about this old Indian ruin except that our friends had said that we *must* see it. What if we went back home and reported that we had been within ten miles of this monument and hadn't gone? On the other hand, we knew by this time that whatever country we passed through would be filled with visions and views we'd never seen before. We would "miss" something else if we *did* go to Mesa Verde. By now we had learned to pay attention to that vague sense that we were being shepherded across the country, guided and protected. And here was this unsolicited advice coming through a cloud of cigarette smoke. We decided on the alternate route and headed for our third and final stop before the ascent.

At the Cortez Safeway, we stocked up on some staples and a relatively light dinner: apples, a melon, a papaya, and a bottle of Zinfandel wine. Then we left town on a road which ran parallel to the mountains. How much longer would we have to prolong the moment of reckoning, I wondered. I felt as though we were doing a little dance around the fringes of the mountains, sidling up to them like a spooky horse skitters around a flapping piece of plastic.

Halfway to Dolores, I happened to look down. My hands were actually shaking on the handlebars! Not since my first piano recital, which sent me running to the bathroom, had I been so excited and nervous. I was a live wire ready to make contact with the great mountains. How steep would the grade be? Would it be snowing up there? Icy? Blizzarding? Could I make it?

DAY 23: Our next day's ride, starting from Dolores, was tricky to plan. We had no idea how far we would be able to ride in these mountains. Our goal was a small town called Telluride at 8,700 feet, sixty-eight miles away. In the Sierra, we'd only been able to make thirty-five to fifty miles in an exhausting day's work. Between Dolores at 6,900 feet and Telluride lay a big unknown. We reckoned with the possibility of having to camp at Lizard Head Pass fifty miles away. Since we rarely camped out if the temperature were going to fall below thirty degrees, we didn't relish this opportunity to snow-camp. There was only one thing to do—go.

The morning was clear and chilly as we wound our way steadily up the mountain through budding aspens and pines, along a clear, swiftly moving stream. Within the bounds of the serious intensity with which I approached the trip, I was happy and relaxed. We stopped for lunch in a ghost town called "Rico." Rico was anything but rich, the lead mine which had provided the economic base for the town having been closed down for many years. The woman who ran the local food shack and general store, the only business in town, was convinced, however, that it was only a matter of a few months before the mine would open up again. Did people in ghost towns never accept the death of their towns? It seemed obvious to us that the place was gone forever, that Rico would eventually be erased from its place on the state maps. Yet the few residents seemed to resist this inevitable demise, this finality.

Over lunch, we watched anxiously as black rolling storm clouds gathered behind us. We pushed on, or rather the wind and the storm pushed us on, up the mountain in high gear. The second uphill tailwind of the trip! Several canyons later, I happily concluded that in Colorado wind traveled upgrade. Carol and I raced on, caught up in the electric spirit of the storm. Except for an occasional ominous sprinkle, however, we beat the storm to Lizard Head Pass. We took a hasty picture of our first Rocky Mountain moment of triumph, then sped down the other side.

In the late afternoon, we sailed into Telluride, dry and high on the unexpected miles we'd made. While we sipped hot tea in a noisy cafe, our bikes leaning against the window, a small group of curious locals gathered to find out what we were about. The population of the little town was young and hip, like a college town. One young man named Alan offered us accommodations at the home of someone whose house he was painting (very generous of him we thought). The promise of a hot shower was like music beckoning; we immediately moved into "Tim's Hotel."

Tim was a rock climber; small, wiry, of Oriental ancestry, a bomb of unreleased energy waiting to assault perpendicular rock walls and overhanging cliffs. I was fascinated by him, by his gear, his preparations, his personality. What makes a mountain climber a mountain climber? I too am a mountain climber—in my dreams and fantasy world. I've struggled up Everest and Annapurna, and scaled the ultimate wall, El Capitan. I've led the successful traverse of the Rock Band on Everest's North Face, rescued fellow climbers trapped in ice crevasses, and taken several near-fatal falls myself. It's a world filled with lofty blizzard-swept peaks that no one has ever seen before, let alone attempted to climb until I did. So I listened and watched Tim closely, feeling his energy, his thrill in planning his next climb. I went with him as he described past ascents.

Carol and I went to dinner at the Tofu Shop where we savored soybean chili, homemade cornbread, salad with sesame dressing, and date bars. Such a treat after the meager diet of soft carrots and limp red cabbage in Northern Arizona! We felt right at home in the little restaurant and natural foods co-op. Fully contented, we walked back through town and were soon sound asleep in our tent pitched in the backyard of Tim's Hotel.

DAY 24: We couldn't have asked for a more brilliant morning as we set out for Montrose sixty-four miles away, on the north side of the Dallas Divide. We were led to the climb by a road which wound gently down a canyon resplendent in shades of copper and lobster, fluttering with born-again aspen trees. I didn't even mind the climb up the Divide, so spectacular was the countryside. We stood in awe of the view at 9,000 feet—an endless panorama of rice-paddy-green valleys surrounded by towering snow-capped peaks. Every second of the day was filled with this magnificent scenery.

The only thing which kept me from fully enjoying the ride was the tension that was mounting between Carol and me. I was really annoyed by how she avoided taking responsibility for making decisions. Whenever we were in a grocery store and I'd ask her what kind of cheese she liked, more often than not it seemed she'd say she didn't care or she'd ask me to choose. I disliked being put in that position; I wanted to avoid making decisions too, or at least avoid making the *wrong* decision. I hated to make mistakes; like the time I persuaded Carol not to put the tent up one night and then it started to rain in the middle of the night. Then I was to blame for the ensuing struggle to put up the tent in a torrent of water and for having to spend the rest of the night in damp sleeping bags.

This fear of doing the wrong thing and taking the consequences had led to a pattern in my life of avoiding any serious statements of choice. I avoided expressions of preference. Statements like "*I* think that's a bad idea," or "*I* don't want to do that," were self-incriminating. If I avoided them, no one could disagree or challenge me, no one could be angry, no one could tell me I was stupid. But I was beginning to see drawbacks to this pattern of evasion. I began to wonder if I had any opinions of my own. I felt that I didn't know what I liked and disliked, what I wanted or didn't want. The more I discovered about who I was, the more I needed to know those things. And the more I was willing to put myself on the line, the more I resented others who wouldn't.

Even though I didn't want to take any chances on ruining our trip and was reluctant to bring up my annoyance with Carol, I could feel myself closing off to her, becoming more and more angry. Carol and I had previously talked about how important it was to share with each other our dislikes and annoyances, to clear the air before it became polluted with resentment. (Still, I didn't want to be the first one to put theory into practice.) So, at lunchtime, I chose a place to stop, next to an old barn, and while the farmer's dog dashed back and forth behind his fence, barking furiously, I told Carol what was bothering me.

I spoke as if my words were raw eggs, trying to remember all I'd been learning about direct interpersonal communications. To my surprise and relief, she didn't seem particularly undone by my criticism; if anything, she was glad that I had said what was bothering me. While we didn't resolve anything, it gave us a chance to bring up some nagging thoughts and clear the air. She'd been harboring a few of her own annoyances. There was a silent understanding between us that we had committed to a two-month marriage, and we were bound and determined to make it work. Making the trip was a fulfillment of a dream for both of us—the most important thing in our lives—and we would do whatever was necessary to make sure it would be completed happily.

After tackling that personal challenge, we began a harried twenty-mile ride to Montrose. I remember thinking, as one of dozens of big trucks skimmed by me, that I hadn't asked for a shave. Funny joke. I was trying to keep a light humor about the whole scene. Better a thwarted sense of humor than to be freaked out that I was eighteen inches from being laid out on the pavement and smashed between Reynolds tubing, National tires and Weinman rims. At that moment, a small herd of deer appeared on top of the levee. They had been drinking in the pond below us and were beginning their return trip to the hills on the other side of the levee road. We jammed on our brakes and watched, spellbound, as the little procession filed over the road. As the last deer skittered down the embankment, the next truck barreled by us.

We received a wonderful surprise in Montrose—a health food store named "Meredith's." Meredith herself, a portly grandmother-type, was on hand to greet us. She put cold apple juice in our hands (organic, unfiltered and natural, of course), and fed us samples of all her best stock. Her store was laid out in fine woods and glass work and was absolutely immaculate. Each item of food was displayed as a piece of art: dried fruit of all kinds and shapes, raw nuts, tamari-roasted nuts, mixed nuts, whole giant cashews—the likes of which I'd never seen before—four sizes of shredded coconut, and an abundance of naturally-sweet treats. After all the 7-11's and Safeway's, we were in Paradise. Showing a total lack of self-restraint, we loaded up on as much food as we could possibly stuff into our packs, pockets and stomachs. Meredith's featured the best granola we'd ever come across. We had given up on the commercial brands, refusing to eat another spoonful no matter how nutritious they claimed to be, so we were especially zealous in our purchase of that item. Our stomachs and packs were bulging by the time we reluctantly walked out the door, wishing there were a Meredith's every 200 miles. Only later, as we hauled each ounce up and over the Continental Divide did we bemoan our over-indulgence.

DAY 25: Due east of Montrose, we began climbing the gradual El Cerro Summit in a road construction zone. Carol's derailleur was again causing problems, slipping in the lowest gear. Now that our route featured upgrades, this was a real problem. Slip . . . skip . . . slip, and every time it slipped, Carol's peace of mind slipped too, and my stomach tightened up another notch. After many skips and slips, it was impossible to hope that it would get better.

We stopped in one of the construction staging areas where engineers and foremen and pieces of huge machinery were rumbling back and forth, back and forth. Carol unloaded Big Blue and turned it upside down on her favorite green shirt so the seat wouldn't be scuffed by the gravel. We got out our tools and our most serious and tense expressions, engaging our analytical, calm minds. Back in Rico, I had noticed that Carol's chain looked awfully loose. Its droop was now almost comical so we took a link out to shorten it. Still something was wrong. The construction crew found us amusing. All the while we were working, we were bombarded with: "A little steep, isn't it girls!" "Where're you going, honey?" We tried, fairly successfully, to ignore it, but inside, we were seething. I wanted to knock somebody's balls up through his skull. One fellow, however, restored our faith in the male sex when he asked us genuinely, "Do you have everything you need?"

We finished our repairs and held our breaths as we pedaled to the top of the grade with not one slip. Inwardly, I glowed, but Carol wasn't going to let her breath out yet (and she was turning blue). We coasted down the other side of the summit, into a dry, almost desert-like area surrounded by rugged rock formations. I was thinking of the Southern California chaparral and times spent at my family's ranch when, alas, slip . . . skip . . . slip . . . . I could see Carol had really had it. She cursed softly and sighed, her nerves as frayed as her gear cable had been in Arizona. We sat down on the shoulder of the road, staring helplessly at the useless derailleur, wondering what the hell we were going to do. As if to answer our prayers, a small, olive-green Mazda station wagon pulled over to the side of the road, and a fatherly Italian emerged from the car with concern written all over his kindly face. Saved again!

Bicycle shops are few and far between in rural America; in fact, we'd not seen a bike store since we'd left Bishop, California, 1,000 miles back, and the outlook for finding one in Western Colorado seemed pretty dim. But another miracle—two even—was waiting for us in the next town forty miles east.

Gunnison, Colorado, was a college town, the site of "Reject U " as the locals called it. No college town would be complete without a bicycle shop, and this one had two of them! Our Italian chauffeur, who had been talking non-stop since we had all squeezed into his car, dropped us off at the door. Carol and I, Little Silver and Big Blue, and the two store mechanics, Chris and Paul, crowded into the back room to study the dilemma. Chris was tall and stocky, an athletic fellow, with "hip" length brown hair and a kind face. Paul was a part-time dentist or part-time bike mechanic, depending on how you looked at it. He was slim and lanky, with a head of balding blond hair which contrasted with a somewhat boyish and playful face. The two partners so clearly enjoyed their enterprise that Carol and I started thinking it would be fun to work in a bike shop when we got home. Chris advised Carol to switch to a more substantial derailleur, one made for mountain climbing and heavy use.

With its shiny new "Sun Tour" derailleur, new chain and free wheel, Big Blue sparkled. (Little Silver was a little jealous.) But Carol refused to be reassured until she had a real road test. She didn't have long to wait; only a half-day's ride away lay the Continental Divide. We spent a pleasant night in a Gunnison motel, dining on an elegant Rondele cheese, crackers and dried fruit.

DAY 26: In the morning we started out with an easy and peaceful twenty miles following a river through farm and rangeland. The sky began to cloud up toward afternoon, as it usually did while we were in the mountains. And then we came to the foot of Monarch Pass, the Continental Divide . . . .

We couldn't see more than a half mile of the ten that would take us up to 11,312 feet. What filled our visual and psychological screen was Mountain, rising steeply from where we stood at a small grocery store at the bottom of the Divide. The shopkeeper advised us of two good rest points on our way up: a picnic area at the two-mile point, and a mountain spring at the five-mile point. We decided to cover the first stretch before lunch; we always liked to have an idea of what we were getting into before relaxing.

Those first two miles were killers. The road rose directly over the foothill at such an impossible grade that I thought, "There's no way I can do this for ten miles!" Every crank took an enormous effort; each revolution I feared would be my last. I had no idea how long I could go, giving so much to climb so little. By the time we arrived at the two-mile mark, I was thoroughly discouraged and depressed. We ate our rice cakes and peanut butter in silence, listening with dismay to the noise on the highway. Trucks and campers coming from above were creeping downhill. They seemed to be going no more than five miles per hour, their motors whining in low gear, straining to hold back the weight of their cargo. Traffic going uphill wasn't moving any faster. We nibbled on a few sardines and an apple. We managed to prolong departure by a number of stalling tactics: pee stops, a squirt of WD-40 on the derailleurs, chain lubricant for Big Blue's new chain, a switch of clothes to get just the right combination of warmth and breathability.

We began again, slowly upward. Still no view of the top. After a half mile, the grade began to even out a bit and in low gear we could keep up a fairly steady climb without becoming exhausted. At the end of the second two miles, we stopped to rest our strained legs, pounding hearts and bulging lungs. We couldn't rest long as the temperature was chilly and the cold quickly penetrated to our joints, stiffening our knees and legs. It hurt to start up again, but after a few minutes of churning upgrade, I got back my pace.

I was anything but bored as I cranked out the inches . . . feet . . . yards . . . fractions of miles. The physical task required all my concentration and determination. I was vaguely aware that the traffic was light, but steady—not much worry there. I felt my body was doing okay, each organ, blood vessel and tiny cell pushed to its limit, but still doing okay. I kept my eyes lowered to within six feet ahead of me; I didn't want to look up and see how far there was to go. Every now and then, however, I would tear my gaze from the road and glance quickly to my right, to the view below. We were making progress. Every inch brought us higher than the second before. The view was slowly expanding, taking in more of the valley below, more of the sky above, and the mountains all around. On a switchback, I could see the road behind us increasing in length. I knew we were making it.

After the seventh mile, I began to feel excited. Carol and Gibi were bicycling over the Continental Divide! All things are possible! I was filled with a sense of wonderment and pride. Cars began to honk, people shouted and waved at us. Others just stared at us in disbelief, which was equally exhilarating. It was hard for me to believe, too. if it weren't for my stiff knees and aching thighs and the steady in-out of my breathing—as far as it would go—I might have thought it was a dream.

We arrived atop the Divide high on pure air and pride. It had been a three-hour climb. I was ecstatic. I felt like a child again. "Whoopee, we made it!" I danced and screamed and hugged Carol, and threw snowballs down the mountains. Carol looked a bit disapproving, but I couldn't and wouldn't contain myself. Some travelers from West Virginia took a Polaroid picture of us as we posed with our bikes under the elevation marker. Another woman wanted our picture to take back home. She kept exclaiming, "I can't believe it!" I hated to go, except the cold began to bite through our cotton T-shirts. We bundled up for the ride downhill.

It remains unknown just how fast a bicycle with thirty-five pounds of gear can travel down a ten percent grade. Let it be enough to say that we were forced to pass a flatbed truck on our way. I was grinning from ear to ear as I chanced a glance at the driver's awestruck face. Ski caps pulled down over our ears, our cheeks bright wind-blown pink, gloved hands working the brakes lovingly—the right amount of squeeze at just the right moment—we flew and never stopped smiling.

We had planned to stop at the first café for a celebration cup of hot tea. A Ramada Inn was not quite the quaint mountain cafe we'd had in mind, but we decided to give it a try. It didn't take long for the Formica decor and the indoor-outdoor carpeting to leave a plastic coating on our jubilant spirits, so we left without our tea. I made a quick telephone call to Tony to inform him of our grand accomplishment. He was appropriately impressed, but even if he hadn't been, it wouldn't have mattered.

We raced on down the mountain and onto the flats. I suddenly became aware that a small band of horses in a roadside pasture were galloping along with us. They snorted at us and pretended to be afraid, using us as an excuse to play. Their manes billowed in the wind, their nostrils flared as they picked up speed and began to overtake us. I could scarcely take my eyes off them. Before long, they reached the end of the pasture where they continued to prance, throw their heads and snort, making a big to-do about the fence that limited their freedom. Intoxicated by their wild pleasure and my own freedom, I pedaled on air the remaining ten miles to Salida.

Salida was unaware of the celebrities who rode into town that evening. Quietly and confidently, we slipped into a booth at a local bar—no need to make a big fuss— and ordered a brandy and white port to toast our success. Our celebration drink was topped off with dinner at Luigi's. We both looked forward to a long, contented sleep.

Salida, Colorado, has two city parks; one is for family picnics and casual Sunday strolls. We camped in the other one at the back side of town. We put up our tent, slipped into our sleeping bags, and wrote briefly in our journals while luxuriously sipping from two miniature bottles of Kahlua bought at the bar. Carol took out her contacts, and we settled down for the night.

I lay awake for a while, thinking ahead to the next day when we planned another rendezvous with Tony in Westcliffe about fifty miles away. Noise and flashing lights woke me. A thunderstorm. I jumped out of my sleeping bag and thrashed around trying to cover the bikes with the flimsy space blanket while the wind tried to strip it off. Back to sleep.

Muffled sounds, ominous and eerie, woke me the second time. My first thought was that Carol was deathly ill and these were the last mortal sounds she would ever utter. But she woke up next to me, said she was okay. We both lay in our sleeping bags, holding our breath, straining to identify the strange noises. They got increasingly louder. My mind flashed to a story I'd read of a couple camping in the woods who were awakened by strange, heavy step sounds in the middle of a moonless night. Not wanting to relive in my own mind the terrors they went through in theirs, I struggled to recall the moral of the story—the worst thing to fear was fear itself; fear breeds inaction which seals one's fate. Yes, that was right. I had to do something, Carol was no help at all. Without her contacts on she was essentially blind. Whatever decisions had to be made or action taken would have to be my responsibility. I hated it; but I hated the thought of dying even more.

Although the sound was still an unearthly moaning and heaving, it was definitely recognizable as human. Feeling as though I were putting my head on the guillotine block, I stuck my head out the tent. The noises, mounting in volume and intensity, were coming from behind our tent. Through the dark, I could make out prone silhouettes rhythmically throbbing on the grass. For all my sexual naïveté, I knew what was going on. Mildly amused, we relaxed and for the third time settled down for the night. But I found myself thinking about the two as I listened to their waning love moans and rustlings in the dark. Was she enjoying herself? Did she want to have sex? Did she feel abused, resigned, raped, proud, mature? How would they feel about each other in the morning? I lay awake remembering my own first clumsy initiation into sex and how cheated I had felt. It wasn't like what the love comics said it would be at all.

DAY 27: We awoke with heavy eyelids, groggy heads, chilled to the bone and slow to energize for the day's ride. Even without midnight lovers, camping out in public places never produced a completely restful sleep. I'd sleep for a brief period, then wake, listening to the local sounds, analyzing them—tones of voices, types of music, animal sounds, the weather. Once I'd reassured myself that all was well, I'd sleep for another short period of time, then reawaken to go through the same process again. It was a disjointed sleep, but it seemed to be sufficient on most nights. The eventful night in the Salida Park, however, had not been restful enough to refuel after the long day's climb over Monarch Pass.

Fortunately, the morning's ride was on a slight downgrade along a river. After we passed through a tall canyon of marbled colors, we had a choice of two different roads going to the same place. We weighed the risks of taking a shortcut that would bypass seven miles of highway. (Memories of the Big Pine shortcut were still alive.) The advantages were obvious—fewer cars, shorter distance, less time. But the thought of grating gravel and deep sand churned my stomach. Nevertheless, from all we could determine from folks at the gas station, it seemed like a harmless enough road, and we decided to take it, despite the vow we had taken never to chance a gravel road again.

It was some distance before I let myself relax. I kept looking far ahead to see when the pavement would change and the dirt road would end. I dreaded each turn. But it was not so bad as I'd feared. The road climbed through magnificent ranch country; the meadow grass was lush green, each pasture surrounded by contrasting pine and sage brush. If I'd seen any "For Sale" signs out, I would have stopped to inquire. True to our good fortune, the weather was perfect, if a bit cool. The sky was a deep, bright blue, sparkling with life, while behind us, over the higher peaks, a spectacular swirling storm was forming, hovering over the snow caps, the shades or black, gray and white mixing like finger-paints.

Inside me, my own storm was brewing. Once again, I wanted to be where I wasn't—at the Westcliffe Airport meeting Tony. We'd agreed to meet at noontime, give or take a few headwinds, mountains, and flat tires. So much can happen to prevent a cross-country biker from getting where she wants to go; and it was all happening to me now. The terrain had become quite hilly—short hills, but steeply graded. And worse, as if on special order, there rose an abominable headwind. I began to scream and curse at the wind, hoping to scare it away. The whole scene was completely predictable. I knew that sooner or later I would have to learn the lesson that I couldn't be in two places at one time. But at the moment, I was still fighting it with everything I had. I was expending so much energy to drive my frustrations and fantasies that my pedaling actually got slower, the headwind became stronger and stronger, the hills steeper and steeper.

At 12 o'clock, still fourteen miles from Westcliffe, we arrived at a little trading post. I walked silently with Carol to the outhouse, peed in silence and fury, and walked silently back with her to our bicycles. I forced myself to tell her that I was having some of my same old problems and that she should ignore my bad mood. Since it was lunchtime, and since we weren't going to arrive in Westcliffe in time for lunch with Tony anyway, I reluctantly suggested we stop here and eat something. I was resigned and crushed, knowing this was the way it had to be.

As we approached the trading post, I looked up from tying my shorts, and there —I could hardly believe my eyes—was Tony! He was standing on the porch, leaning on a post like Matt Dillon, with a big green Hertz-colored station wagon "hitched" to the rail. Was this a dream? No one else could possibly fit the description—green plaid Vyella shirt, khaki pants, blond balding head, wire rim glasses—it had to be Tony. I was beside myself with joy and relief. We hugged and hugged, stared at each other for long moments. We hugged some more. I felt a little sheepish about falling into such good fortune. I didn't deserve to get off so easily. Now I wouldn't have to test my resolve of patience and living in the present moment for fourteen miles. It didn't take long to stop feeling guilty, however, sailing along at 55 mph, with not a trace of headwind or a steep grade.

We found a secluded campsite in the San Isabel Forest at the foot of the Sangre de Cristo mountains and celebrated our reunion with our first real campfire, several bottles of wine, and some Jiffy popcorn.

DAY 28: We lounged around camp, looked at pictures of the trip that Tony had taken at Lake Mead, played "Hearts" while a light snow fell, caught up on news, and opened mail. Carol's friend Arthur had sent her a very sporty biking jersey and a pair of shorts. The jersey was light blue and maroon striped, and Carol looked very snappy in it. She was embarrassed to wear it, however, because it looked too professional, so she didn't show it off much during the trip. (Tony took a picture of her in that shirt which I later enlarged and keep on my desk at home. Looking at it brings memories to my mind and tears to my eyes. I never look at it very long because the emotion that wells up inside me is overwhelming and huge.) The biking shorts were too big for Carol, so I claimed them, happy to be out of my wool shorts, and happy I could fit into a smaller pair of shorts. This was a source of some pleasure, my obsession with losing weight being what it was.

We pitched our tents close to the little stream that ran through the campground. Carol worried about being so close to the stream; she fantasized that in the middle of the night a flash flood would strike and we'd all be washed away. It was a tiny little stream, not likely to rise up into a raging Rio Grande, so we teased and laughed about it. I loved her for her little paranoias, and would have jumped into the flood after her if she'd been washed away.

Tony and I were sound asleep, curled together in our double sleeping bags, when we were awakened by a small, urgent voice outside our tent. "Tony, Gibi, it's raining! Do you think we'll be okay?" I paused to listen to the faint patter coming down on our tent before reassuring her that I was positive we were safe. I could hardly blame her for being nervous. After all, with no contacts on she was blind as a bat. In that condition, better to ask than sit around and wait for the deluge to come.

DAY 29: After another relaxed day around camp, and a tour of Westcliffe, we spent the night in a town motel so that Tony could leave early in the morning to catch his flight from Denver. It wasn't so hard this time to have him leave, but still . . . these nights together had been so warm and secure.

The Plains

I do not know where Kansas is, for I have never heard that country mentioned before. But tell me, is it civilized country?

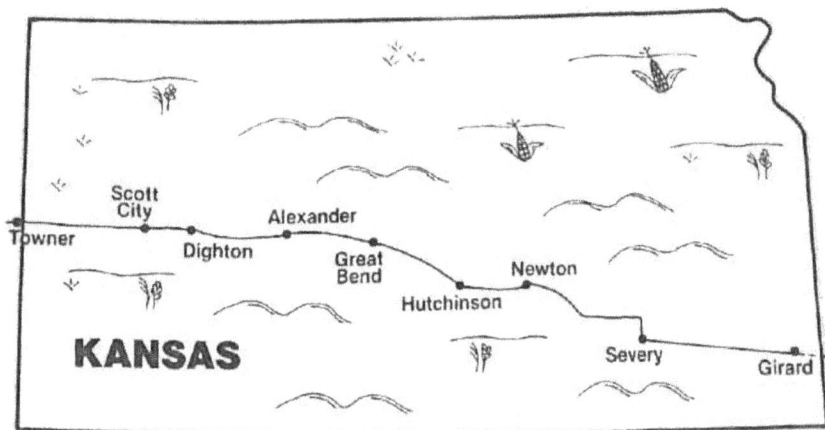

DAY 30: Carol and I set off early, too. We climbed that sparking morning for several miles east of Westcliffe, then rolled onto the most gorgeous downhill of the whole trip. An 8% grade—we didn't have to ride our brakes all the time—easy racing curves, slightly banked but not too steep, a satin-smooth road surface with ample room for bikes, no traffic and magnificent scenery. We arrived in Pueblo fifty-two miles and five hours later, having said our final farewells to the Rockies.

Pueblo was a sprawling, sand city filled with shopping centers and 7-11 stores. We spent part of the afternoon changing tires in front of the Laundromat. Tony had brought me a new tire from the bike shop back home to replace my worn rear tire. Carol switched hers from front to back, expecting to complete the journey on one set of tires. That was one expectation that was met. We gathered some groceries and left for the Plains, another big unknown and formidable part of our journey.

By seven that evening we were in another world. It was a shock to have moved into another landscape in just twenty-three miles. We arrived in Boone, Colorado, and set up our camp in the "city park" next to the local tavern. Strains of the Beatles and Bobby Darin coming from the open bar door caught us up in memories of the 50's as we settled in for the night.

I was sound asleep when my blind partner roused me. "Is that a man sitting in front of that tree looking at us?" Carol was looking straight ahead, out the open tent flap, completely rigid and intent on the night beyond our tent. I lay there, stunned. (Goodbye Mother, Dad, Tony. It's been a nice trip. I've enjoyed my short stay here on earth. Hope to see you again . . . .) If there *was* a man staring at us in our tent, what was he thinking about? What was he going to do? Why would someone sit looking at two sleeping girls in the middle of the night? Was he some pervert concocting the most ghastly, vile crime ever yet committed against women? As long as he sits there, I thought gloomily, there was nothing we could do, and we sure couldn't go to sleep. We were cows in a feedlot, getting fat and flush with fear-flowing blood, moist with adrenalin-pumped sweat. How juicy that would make us! How desirable! Okay, Fear, that's enough. It's time for Courage and Action to take over. I opened my eyes, said a last prayer and sat up to look out the tent.

It was totally black outside. I strained to see the tree six feet in front of our tent, hoping to God that I wouldn't see anything but the trunk. I squinted, changed eyes, opening and closing to get different perspectives, but I couldn't make out any misplaced from or grotesque creature sitting in front of the tree. Carol wanted to go pee. I withheld my final verdict for several more seconds, because I hated the thought of sending my helpless friend out to pee on top of the local maniac. Finally, I pronounced, "It looks all right to me. I can't see anything." I held my breath as she crawled out of the tent and disappeared behind the tree. Why did she always have to go to the bathroom after we had gone to bed? I fumed, anxiously awaiting her return. When she reappeared and had snuggled back into bed, I relaxed a little, but the specter continued to haunt me into the early morning hours.

DAY 31: I woke up determined to identify and fix the clicking noises I'd been hearing in my rear wheel ever since I'd changed my tires in Pueblo I'd tried unsuccessfully to ignore it. After breakfast, I flipped Little Silver on its seat and reset the rear wheel. It seemed to me that the free wheel was wiggling too much around the axle, and that the rear wheel was out of true. The last thing I was going to attempt to do was true my own wheel. Once, with Gerry's help, I had tried to straighten out a crooked wheel by myself and ended up turning a perfectly good wheel into a "Spaghetti-O" from a can of "Alpha-bit" soup. Our guide book showed us that we would come to a bike store in Kansas within a couple of days. I resolved to try to live with the persistent noises until then, and we pushed on.

The Plains were flat and plain; no doubt about it. The constancy of the biking here made it particularly difficult. Everything was the same: road surface, elevation (flat), scenery, wind and sky. No change at all. At least in the desert I'd had various emotional traumas to preoccupy my mind, and the landscape had its special kind of beauty. This was a visual desert. We ran out of trees after Sugar City and ran head-on into the ill-reputed southeasterly winds.

In response to the bleakness of the outer world, my inner resources came to the rescue. I began to sing to myself. First, soundless hummings deep inside of me; then some tentative, quiet, musical mutterings; then out loud, full-fledged singing. My pace and a tune would find each other, and I would sing it over and over and over. "Good King Wenceslas," Tony's favorite Christmas carol, fit eastern Colorado perfectly. The Good King and I got to be very good friends—one word for each pedal stroke. To my great satisfaction, this form of entertainment worked beautifully, a meditation that kept me moving contentedly through the Plains for many empty hours. It proved to be not only an essential discipline, but also the beginnings of a new and wonderful experience for me—I re-discovered music.

I'd started playing the piano at my parents' request when I was five years old. For medical reasons, I needed to exercise my right hand which was then very tiny and without much muscle or coordination. I am told it looked a little like a chicken claw, although I don't remember it being that ugly. So I started playing (and typing, bouncing balls, and shaking hands vigorously) and continued through high school. My classical piano was pretty good by then. But whenever I practiced downstairs in the huge pink and white living room on the glossy black, baby grand piano, the two giant doors were closed behind me, just as the kitchen door was closed on the smells of sautéing onions. When I was requested to play before my family from time to time, I was always mortally embarrassed, terrified to perform because I was so afraid of making bad sounds and mistakes. Everybody was surprised by my shyness since I played so well.

I remember, too, one night as a child, lying awake, singing and singing— quietly, so that I wouldn't keep Tory awake in the next room. But someone heard me and came to shush me up. "No noise," I was remonstrated. "Don't raise your voice, dear." I dutifully squelched my singing, my voice, my noise. The consequences of not doing so were too painful.

So here in bleak eastern Colorado, that little voice was trying to escape again. It became bolder and bolder as the miles went by, and I expanded my repertoire to include "Man of La Mancha," "The Impossible Dream," "Stormy Weather," "Young Lovers," and "Blue Bayou." "The Impossible Dream" became my theme song – the words fit so well to my moods, my fears, my hopes, my determination.

> To dream the impossible dream,
> To fight the unbeatable foe,
> To bear with unbearable sorrow,
> To run where the brave dare not go . . .

I sang my way past grain elevators, ghost towns, wind-swept, eroded fields, feedlots ripe with the smell of cow dung, urine and death.

> This is my quest:
> To follow that star
> No matter how hopeless
> No matter how far . . .

The 125 miles to Kansas were the bleakest and hardest of the whole trip. Our spirits and energy were at rock bottom when we pulled into a dusty town called Haswell that second night in post-Rockies Colorado. We camped in what might have been called a city park, although the grass was long and barely green, the picnic table splintery and off-balance. But we had running water from a pump, and even the table was a luxury to us by the time we arrived, depressed and tired. As we ate dinner, we were vaguely aware of several cars "cruising," even in Haswell.

After we'd retired for the night, we began to sense that there was more to this cruising than first met our eyes. A young boy, about fourteen, appeared at our tent and asked if we'd seen his dog. (The famous "lost my dog" story, I thought, already suspicious.) Apparently it had been lost for so long that he couldn't describe it for us. Casually, he asked us a few questions about where we were from, who we were, where we were going and then left.

Ten minutes later, three cars full of beer-drinking "townies" pulled up behind our tent. "Hey, man, there're *girls* in that tent! Let's go see if they want to party." I kept hearing the *fft, ffft* of popping beer can tops, punctuating the laughing and whispering. For long seconds it was quiet, then, "Come on, girls, at least stick your heads out the back so we can see you." (This was impossible as the back flap was sewn shut). When we finally spoke, it was to plead exhaustion and need of sleep. They weren't persuaded, however, and they weren't going away. That much was clear. We were very tired and getting increasingly anxious. In a show of courage and boldness that surprised me I pulled on my shorts and T-shirt and climbed out of the tent.

About five (or was it ten?) tough-looking, or trying-to-be-tough-looking kids were in each car, all guzzling beer with extra six-packs by their sides. Most of them were wearing cut-off denim shirts, which revealed budding adolescent biceps and menacing tattoos. Glittering sets of braces on their teeth made them look even more adolescent, but nonetheless intimidating. I turned myself into a turtle—cool, calm and confident. On the inside I was quaking. My demeanor fooled them. Remembering Gerry's coaching on how to handle tough situations, I answered their questions in a friendly, matter-of-fact way, as if this were the most common of circumstances for me. They took a certain amount of delight in telling me that the wind, that had come up after dinner and was now blowing like a gale, would blow that way for days. (It *was* the fiercest, most exhilarating windstorm I'd ever seen.) I explained that we'd come seventy miles that day and were exhausted. "Normally," I lied, "we'd be up for some socializing, but just not tonight." I stood there after my speech, wondering helplessly what would happen next, whether they would buy my excuse. Miraculously, they bought it and said they "wouldn't keep me any longer." I quelled my momentary rage at that presumptuous comment and walked back to the tent, relieved but still tense. After another nerve-racking fifteen minutes, they gunned their engines and screeched around the corner to be swept up in the wind. Where I got the courage and presence of mind I don't know. It wasn't like me at all. I lay awake for some time, rerunning the scenes, the conversation, and listening to the raging wind.

DAY 32: We woke up to the same blasting wind. Jesus, would it *ever* stop? If I didn't have to bike in it, I would have thoroughly enjoyed its fury. Even Carol was discouraged. We set off at a slow, demoralized pace, making ten miles to Eads where we stopped for breakfast. The cafe was filled with local farm folk and we learned plenty about the area and the people by listening to their conversations about farm equipment, weather, and the latest rash of equipment thefts. The Spanish omelet and blueberry pie upset both our stomachs for the rest of the day. I passed most of the blank hours singing the Beatles' song, "Oh blah dee, oh blah da . . . ."

On our last night in Colorado, we stopped in Towner where I called Tony from a phone booth that had no glass in it; we could barely hear each other for the wind that blew into the telephone. We asked the local postmistress, who had stepped outside her office for a moment, where we might camp. She became more and more uneasy as we chatted with her. Finally, she turned and fled into her house, which was also the post office, pleading "burning cookies." We would have been delighted to help her dispose of any charred homemade cookies, but she never returned to offer us any. We went across the street to the "park" and had a miserable supper of pretzels, rubbery carrots and leftovers.

DAY 33: Kansas was a dismal prospect. I imagined endless miles of wheat, corn, soy fields and feedlots. Our fantasies and fears had been molded by people we'd met along the way; sometimes their eyeballs would roll into their heads at the mere thought of biking across Kansas, and sometimes they'd just give us pitying glances. We would either hate it or despise it.

But then others told us how hospitable Kansans were. And one group of bikers guaranteed us fast riding on strong westerly winds. Now a feature like *that* could make Hades look like Yosemite. Whatever it was, it was unknown. We were leaving the West, our home, for a mystery land. We set out to cross the border under threatening skies, pedaling hard to reach Tribune, Kansas, before it rained.

To my surprise, I found myself totally caught up in delightful fantasy. I was on the Yellow Brick Road on my way to the Land of Oz. In the distance the silver grain elevator of the town of Tribune rose majestically into the misty gray early morning sky—the Wizards Castle. What would I ask of the Wizard when *I* reached Oz? Love? Patience? Tolerance? That sounded corny, but I felt at the time needy of those qualities.

Three miles out of Tribune, the rain interrupted my fantasy. The dread prospect had at last arrived—our first storm on the road. We pulled out our Gortex rain gear, finally able to test its claims to both rain protection and breathability. We pedaled on furiously, trying to reach shelter as soon as possible.

Normally, I love the rain. Being a native of drought-stricken California where rain is a precious commodity, I am always happy when it comes. During my childhood, my father and I would take special long walks together in the rain at our family's ranch outside Los Angeles. We'd slop in the mud to the Waterfall, crossing over the torrent of water that came down through the fields to watch and wonder at the roar of water that fell over the rocks. Or we would sit in the living room by the fire and watch the rain, absorbing it with the same appreciation and gratitude that I imagine the plants and grasses did. And when it came down in sheets, so gray and thick we could see no more than twenty feet away, we would get up and go outside to stand under the porch, watching and listening, silently giving thanks for the heavens' gift. I liked the rain because it was pretty and different from the usual sunny Southern California skies. To my father, it meant the well-being and productivity of the ranch. The rain became important to me because I knew it was important to him, and although mine was a childlike appreciation, we both loved it equally.

But on the road I saw rain as a catalyst to all kinds of experiences and encounters I wanted to avoid. I imagined the parts on my bike gritting, rusting and wearing down. Breaking down out on the road seemed to me like such a major catastrophe. Why was it, I pondered, that we two women had such trepidation about mechanical failures, when the young men cyclists we'd met saw those problems as just another part of their biking adventure? Why did they look upon repairs, untrue wheels, thorns in tubes as fun and not as trauma? To us, mechanical failure was an awesome, almost insurmountable mountain; to those young men it was barely a hill. They talked about such problems with gusto and pleasure: "You wouldn't have *believed* the shape my wheel was in! . . . ha, ha, ha." Here *we* were, three miles from breakfast, squinting, blinking, grimacing in the face of a little rain storm. (I don't screw up my face in the shower, so why in the rain, I wondered.)

We arrived at the Feedlot Cafe, gritty, wet, gloomy and chilled, inside and outside. The bathroom was the warmest spot in the whole place, and we were tempted to spend the rest of the morning in there, huddled next to the hot water heater.

We were sitting at our table by the window, curled around mugs of hot tea, waiting for something to put in our stomachs when Cy Higgins, chairman of the bicentennial Bikecentennial in Kansas interrupted our wet, steamy thoughts with a Kansas greeting. All I wanted was to be left alone with my own gloom. But how could we refuse the company of a local Kansan? We invited him to join us, and he sat down, ordered himself a cup of coffee and pulled out his pack of cigarettes.

Reluctantly we were drawn into conversation with him, but soon found ourselves interested and eager to know more about who he was, what he did, where he lived—the hell with the cigarette smoke. He wanted to know the same about us. Carol expressed our interest in the operation of the grain elevators which so dominated the landscape. Before we knew it, we were following Cy out the door for a personally conducted tour of the Tribune grain elevator. We were concerned about leaving our bicycles and gear untended but Cy assured us, as we climbed into his pickup, that in Kansas – and nowhere else in the country—they would be perfectly safe.

The grain elevator, while interesting, was not as dramatic as I'd expected, and the elevator itself was out of order so we couldn't get to the top to see the stored grain or the view of the surrounding countryside. I was a little disappointed, but Cy's hospitality and generosity made up for it. We were having a tour of a real Kansas grain elevator with a genuine Kansas farmer! I tentatively broached the subject of organic farming versus chemical agribusiness and was delightedly surprised when he said that "all a farmer needs is a little rain and some lightning for nitrogen, and the crops'll grow jest fine." That was even more organic than I'd imagined.

We were touched by Cy's folksy manner and easy familiarity. Well, I thought, maybe it's true what they say about Kansans . . . . I left Tribune with visions of being a farmer, although it was mind-boggling to think how one farmer could manage such vast acres of farmland. I saw myself riding on my tractor through endless fields of wheat, hauling grain to the grain elevator, waiting in line—like a gas line—to unload my harvest, tending the hogs, cattle and chickens, putting up vegetables for the winter, sitting around the fireplace quilting, or making repairs on the farm machinery, going to the local bar on a Saturday night to drink and talk with the other farmers about the year's crop, the weather, the new brand of feed.

Carol stopped suddenly, after only ten minutes on the road, complaining of severe leg pains. Since a little physical pain never stood in the way of making our daily miles, I knew when she stopped and began massaging her thigh, looking worried and pained, that it was no small inconvenient muscle spasm. She tried to keep riding, but had to stop every 100 yards to rub her thigh and knee. We tried wrapping an Ace bandage around the sore area and stopped repeatedly to reposition it, but it brought only minimal relief. Carol was more upset by not understanding the cause of the pain than from the actual discomfort of it. She was also starting to feel guilty about holding up our parade.

We limped along for the next forty-five miles. I was excruciatingly frustrated at not being able to bike at the pace I and my body were accustomed to going. We had agreed at the beginning of the trip to always stay in sight of the other person, curves and high speed permitting. It was also important for Carol's morale at that point to have company in sight. So we made a great pair, midway between Tribune and Scott City, Kansas: she, guilty; I, frustrated.

I've never been a particularly patient person, and I can be very spoiled. When I set something in mind, I want to act on it immediately and be gratified immediately. I trace most of this attitude back to my upbringing in a wealthy family. Materially speaking, I was never wanting. There were few times when I didn't have what I wanted when I wanted it; usually I had more than I wanted before I even dreamed I wanted it. I never knew what working hard for anything meant; it seemed that things just happened. I didn't have to and couldn't do anything.

On top of that, I had the attitude of what I call a "woman-in-waiting." I, like most women, was raised to wait for life to happen to me: we little girls wait for Daddy to come home from work, we wait for our big brothers to play with us, we wait for Mommy to buy us a new dress or stick of lipstick, wait until our dream boy (or the drippiest guy in the neighborhood—take what you can get) asks us to the dance, wait for compliments and praise to come our way, wait to meet the right man who will marry us, and wait for him to come home at night. We don't feel that we have the capabilities or the permission to make life happen the way *we* want it to happen, to ask for what we want, to change what we don't like. Here on the Yellow Brick Road, I wasn't getting what I wanted—there was no way I could—and my frustration was quickly reaching an intolerable level.

After a few miles of churning my pedals in low gear and riding on top of Carol's rear wheel, I finally reckoned with the realities of my situation. There wasn't any way I could go quickly; the frustration was all mine. It struck me that another person might be perfectly happy to have such a good excuse to slow down and enjoy the scenery. I knew it was up to me to make the ride pleasant, although it was difficult to see how to at that point or even to see that I wanted to. It was far easier and more customary to fixate myself in my helpless, miserable situation. Woe is me! But I surprised myself, as I had on several previous occasions, and took a great leap out of my hole.

My first strategy was to drop back a quarter of a mile behind Carol. I estimated her pace so that I wouldn't gain or lose ground but could keep exactly the same rhythm: pump, pump, pump . . . . (Oh, this was going to be hard!) Then I brought out my singing voice and scrounged around for as many songs as I could possibly remember, plus a few old camp songs, some school cheers and the faithful "Good King Wenceslas." At first, I sang quietly to myself, and then, since I was far enough away so Carol couldn't hear me and there was no one else around—unless you count cows and wheat—I squeaked forth a few tunes out loud, becoming bolder and louder, until presently I was a veritable Julie Andrews.

From time to time I'd stop and take pictures. I framed the boundless fields of green wavin' wheat; old, gray, weather-worn barns; and silver-shiny silos. The happier

I became (i.e., the less frustrated) the more beautiful Kansas became. By the end of the day, I was astounded at the rare good mood I was in.

We spent the night in a Scott City motel, watching television and recovering from fanny fatigue—the result of our slower pace. Most of the TV stations concentrated on weather reports; the various weather dials told us all we needed to know about what was important to the people of Kansas: not the Middle East crisis, nor the election campaigns in California, nor court decisions on discrimination—just farming.

DAY 34: The morning was cloudy and chilly and we had to bundle up as if we were crossing the Sierra again. I had taken the lead—a rare occasion—and was listening with increasing concern to Little Silver's clicking noises. Contrary to what our Bikecentennial guidebook told us, there was no bike shop in Scott City. I tried my best to keep my anxiety under control, knowing that somewhere in Kansas, we would find what we needed.

As we rode, I began to day dream about my VISTA days, some nine years before. It dawned on me that the pre-school children I'd taught were now between twelve and fourteen years old! I'd never forgotten one Chicano boy named Tomas. I was very fond of him and admired his spirit (which was seen most of the time as bullying), but keeping a handle on him consumed so much of my time and energy that eventually I had to kick him out of school. It startled me to realize he was now a streetwise teenager in East L.A. What effect had I had on his life? Was my kicking him out of school the first of many rejections which would permanently lock him out of the white culture? Was he stealing? Shooting heroin? In jail? I was so absorbed in my reflections that I didn't realize I had quickened my pace and Carol was out of sight.

I stopped and waited for her to catch up. The pain in her leg had started again after a few miles, and it was obvious that we would have to cut the day short. We pulled in behind the wall of a country elementary school to escape the wind and discuss what to do. She was as frustrated with her pain as I was with the slow pace. And she was feeling very guilty. I spoke honestly when I told her that while I was frustrated with our slow pace, I would still rather be here—in Kansas, with her, on my bicycle—than anywhere else.

Sitting with our backs to the warm stucco wall, we unwound our frustration and guilt, and the choices we had for our day became clearer. Flying home was out of the question. Renting a car to drive to Wichita for a movie was not possible for the lack of rent-a-car agencies in the nearby vicinity. Hitching a ride to Great Bend where there was a bike store would be a 100-mile "cheat." We could ride s⁄l⁄o⁄w⁄l⁄y to Dighton, only eight excruciating miles farther and stop there for the day. There was an element of disgrace in both of the last two options. Hitching was taking the easy way out. After all, if it wasn't hard, it must not be legitimate. (Where on earth did we pick up such notions?) But it was equally disgraceful to have only biked twenty-four miles in three and a half hours! Except for the day climbing in the Sierra, we'd never gone less than fifty miles a day, and, of late, we'd been averaging sixty-five. We decided to put off the final decision until we reached Dighton.

Upon our arrival, we treated ourselves—Carol to fruit and I to fresh-popped popcorn and two green peppers. Sitting in the supermarket parking lot, soaking up the sun as it bounced off the concrete wall and the asphalt, our spirits began to pick up. As she crunched a green apple, Carol said, "You know, this trip is supposed to be *fun*. We shouldn't be so hard on ourselves." I nodded my head, silently ruminating over that idea.

Just as we were accepting that it might be okay to slow down a little, an offer dropped from the clearing Kansas sky. A young blond man walked up and asked if we might like to spend the night at his house. (What would Mother say?!) Jim Newsom and his dad were owners of the supermarket. He explained he was on his way to a golf tournament in Scott City and wouldn't be back until later that evening, so the house would be ours; we could shower, fix dinner, and make ourselves at home.

We were incredulous at his kind offer. Still undecided about hitching to Great Bend (we wondered whether there was a movie theatre there), we thanked him for the invitation and said we'd let him know as soon as we had made up our minds. The decision involved very complex issues for us. Jim seemed like a pretty straight fellow, honest and trustworthy; and the town *did* look nice; and the grocery store was more than adequate for our needs. But we'd only gone twenty-four miles! It seemed to me there was something in our situation to learn from; something about relaxing a little, not working and pushing so hard. We might enjoy seeing the countryside, meeting some local people. After all, that was what Kansas was all about, wasn't it?

We accepted Jim Newsom's invitation. But as soon as we got into his bright yellow Corvette to drive to his house, we began to have second thoughts. You could count on one hand the number of Kansans who had sports cars, let alone Corvettes. Who was this guy, anyway? He had a small ordinary house at the end of a quiet street on the edge of town. (Town stretched two blocks in all directions from the center.) When he opened the front door, we were faced with an array of poster-size nudes and stacks of back issues of *Playboy* and *Oui* magazines. Had my intuition failed me? Still, he seemed harmless—even innocent. We moved our bikes and ourselves in for the night.

For all the trappings of a macho jock, Jim was a quiet, kind and generous man. He offered Carol and me the use of his king-size bed for the night (what bliss that would have been!), but we felt that was taking too much and stretched our sleeping bags out on the living room floor. He had one housemate—a two-month old kitten, all white and squeaky, which he had raised himself from a bottle after the mother was killed. We were reassured. He returned to town to buy us two bottles of Lancers and a corkscrew, then roared off to his golf tournament.

It was June 2nd, and Carol and I discovered another of a remarkable number of coincidental connections between us; her father and my mother were born sixty-one years earlier on that same day. In the early evening, we walked the mile into town to the Dighton Hotel to make birthday phone calls.

The hotel was as well-established as its owners, Mary and Paul Downing, who looked to be in their seventies. They soon recognized us as a willing audience and began to tell us about their special hobby—handcrafting models of horse-drawn carriages hitched to toy horses. Proudly, they brought out some of their most treasured and prize-winning facsimiles, climbing to the highest storeroom shelves to retrieve them. Along with this hobby, Mary made ornaments and figures from woven wheat.

Enchanted with her unique creations, I asked if I could buy two of them. She hesitated, thinking they weren't good enough to sell. Just a little pastime, she said, not worth anything. I assured her that I would have expected to pay at least $20 for the golden heart tied with red satin ribbon that I wanted; she was embarrassed to ask for $1.75. I bought a woven wheat "J" for Tom and Paula Jorde, and sent the wheat heart, along with love from my own, to Tony. Kansas was getting better all the time.

Back at Jim's we watched color TV, drank wine, and I ate junk food out of his kitchen closets. His cupboards were a gold mine of pink marshmallowy cookies and Mal-o-Mars Cookies, my childhood favorite—chocolate-covered marshmallow sponges that disintegrate before you have to chew them. There was also deliciously sticky, lemon custard ice cream in the freezer which I could feel oozing into my body, gumming up all the works like glue. It was the kind of ice cream that hardens in the bowl if it sits out at room temperature long enough. I spooned large globs into my eager mouth, alternating between feelings of guilt and embarrassment and pure bliss.

Jim returned in a great fanfare of engine revving, and we all watched television and talked about our trip. He was genuinely curious and interested—impressed, too—and was particularly surprised that we hadn't been hassled by men. (Would he be the first?) He was amused by our pure diet (hah!) of fresh fruits, raisins, granola. At one point during the evening, without saying a word, he left and sped off in his car. He returned shortly with bags full of grapes and apples and raisins from his supermarket for us to take on our journey. I was amazed at such generosity, particularly since I was the object of it. By the time we turned in for the night, both Carol and I felt relaxed and assured of our situation.

After a couple of hours—it must have been midnight—we were awakened by a loud banging on the front door. Several of Jim's buddies called out to him to open up; they wanted to join the party. Word of our arrival at his house had spread quickly in the small town. As the banging on the door grew louder, my imagination put the pieces together. Jim was probably one of the few bachelors in town. If that were the case, the posters and magazines began to make sense—his house was the local hangout. I envisioned the living room filled with cigarette smoke, empty beer cans piled up on the table, raucous laughter rising from the small group of horny Dighton jocks.

Sleepily, Jim stumbled from his room, stepped over our bags, and told his pals through the locked door that yes, there were two girls here (no, *not* three) and that we were asleep (you bet your ass we weren't!). He told them there would be no party tonight and said goodnight. He stepped back over our sleeping bags, apologizing for the disturbance, and went back to his bedroom.

Twenty minutes later, there came more banging at the front door, more laughter and loud voices. The scenario repeated itself, Jim talking through the locked door: "Yeah, they're on bicycles." ("Bet they have some pretty nice thighs!") "No, they don't want a beer." As he stumbled back over our bags for the fourth time, he was obviously chagrined and exasperated with his fun-loving friends.

His friends, however, were not yet completely discouraged. At 2:30 in the morning, they made another attempt to start a party. They beat on both the front door and back doors simultaneously, then left. Fifteen minutes later, mini-fireworks began exploding around the house. Exhausted as I was, I had to laugh. It was only when the fireworks subsided and the night became quiet again that I took stock of our vulnerable and precarious position.

DAY 35: We allowed ourselves a leisurely 10:30 departure after two huge mugs of tea and extensive journal writing. The air gave all the signs of approaching summer – it was cloudy and humid, insects hummed in the tall grass; a lazy summer-sticky morning. Carol's leg was finally healed, and we biked along side-by-side for hours, over the Smoky Hills Region where the hills roll gently, the grasses are lush and the wind barely whispers. We talked about our relationships with Tony and Arthur and other men, about Arthur joining us for the last week of the trip, feminism, ourselves, and the previous night's events. We felt a strong and growing bond between us, a mutual trust and respect. Taking care of each other's needs had become our first concern. Besides myself, Carol was the most important person in my world at that moment, a discovery which surprised and pleased me.

I had first noticed the strength of this bond during our stay at Jim Newsom's house. In times past, all my attention would have been directed at Jim, the all-important Male: how do I look, how am I coming across, does he like me? Instead, I found myself thinking about how *Carol* was feeling, what *she* wanted, whether *she* was happy. Suddenly, there was something more important in my life than a man! What a shock. What a pleasant surprise. My whole life had been blindly oriented to attracting and securing the appreciation and admiration of the male sex. Always, I was aware of and concerned about the men around me, even if they were of no consequence and my efforts to attract them were totally inappropriate. Somehow I knew that, but didn't seem able to stop or change my behavior. Now my world had changed; I had broken out of this psychological prison. It had been Carol, not Jim. I was free.

Time passed quickly. It was the very first day that I didn't care about where we were on the map, how far we had gone, or what the mileage markers on the road read. It was a momentous feeling—the "be here now" was finally happening. Our fanatical compulsion to Move Forward Fast was fading, and already we'd been blessed with the rewards of a slower pace. I was in heaven as we rode out of Ness City on a real Red Brick Road. The country seemed to get more and more lush and beautiful. I could ride here forever. It was almost sacrilegious to be enjoying Kansas so much after all the terrible things we'd been told. Great expectations . . . small expectations. *No* expectations.

Our nights, however, continued to be more eventful than restful. What with tent-side lovers, fantasies of faceless men peering into our tent, cruising townies and fireworks, sleep was becoming less and less frequent. Add to those events barking dogs, bright street lamps, thundering freight trains and midnight rain storms, and sleep nearly became an endangered species. On our thirty-fifth night, we camped at a roadside rest-stop in Alexander, Kansas. We confidently concluded that, because it had been such a fine day, it would be perfectly safe to sleep under the stars, tucked underneath some trees. That suited me. I much preferred sleeping in the open if I could, and not having to put the tent up.

It was a fine rain that woke Carol who stumbled over to my sleeping bag— irritated—and woke me up out of a sound sleep. We fumbled and fumed, setting up the tent, and were thoroughly wet by the time we were finished. Not only was everything damp in the morning, but Little Silver had come through the night with its second flat tire. The message was echoing loud and clear: slow down . . . slow down . . . slow down . . . take each day as it comes . . . don't worry about the miles. By the time the four of us were in shape to ride, it was noon. We set off at a brisk pace, and a half hour later Big Blue had a flat.

By mid afternoon, we'd barely managed twenty miles. In a light drizzle, we took refuge under a deserted gas station roof somewhere in central Kansas. We were gazing into the gray mist when a patrol car pulled into the station. The sheriff was looking for a tornado, spotted locally, and the two young bike-touring Englishmen with him were looking for us. They had heard of Carol and me some 100 miles west and had pedaled like crazy to catch up, thinking we would make delightful traveling companions. Two girls – wow! I was sorry for their disappointment when they discovered we were not at all keen on traveling with anybody, especially men. We were reluctant to break our routine and tight bond; I felt selfish, inflexible – and certain about that. Tight as Carol and I felt, however, we did enjoy cycling toward Great Bend with our fellow bikers for a few hours in the late afternoon.

About six, I had the third flat tire of the day, which was good only in that it revealed the cause of one of Little Silver's problems. The bike store at home had given Tony a defective tire which I'd put on in Pueblo, and it had finally split, leaving the tube exposed to gravel, thorns, heat and asphalt. It was more than any tube could stand. The demise of that tire, however, didn't happen in the Middle of Nowhere; it happened 100 feet from a shopping center on the outskirts of Great Bend, Kansas, the first city with a bike store since Gunnison, Colorado, 570 miles back! Our mysterious "Divine Spirit" obviously was still with us. I put a temporary bandage on my tire while Carol and the English bikers went to the supermarket. The contents of their respective bags of supper fixings were amusing: ours filled with raw vegetables and hot mustard; theirs with raw hamburger, buns and instant mashed potatoes.

That evening, Carol and I watched the third in the "Eleanor and Franklin" TV series and found another common bond. Eleanor Roosevelt was a heroine and model for both of us. The program, which captured Eleanor's spirit, her strength and her dedication to social justice, moved us deeply, and we reflected on our own lives and our trip. Our experience with Jim Newsom and his bachelor buddies had made Carol feel that we ought to be slowing down even more than we were so that we could meet people on more than a superficial level. I agreed with her that one way to make a cross-country trip would be to make a concerted effort to "meet people," to share ideas and beliefs. (Both of us would have liked talking with Jim Newsom about the Women's Movement, because it was certainly true that one purpose of the trip for me was to prove the competency and independence of women.) Yet I knew that—to the extent that we wanted to influence how people viewed women—we were making a deep impression just by what we were doing. We were our own political and philosophical statement, free-wheeling across America, bandaged tire and all.

DAY 36: In the morning I tended to my bicycle needs at a shop owned by a middle-aged couple who were exceedingly uninterested in our travels. Our British friends had arrived at the shop earlier, and perhaps the owners felt overrun by a bunch of know-it-all kids. The owner coolly diagnosed the problem in Little Silver's rear wheel as a malfunction of my brand new Phil Wood hub. Since the hub was sealed (supposedly one of its best features), it was impossible to inspect it inside. I felt I had little choice but to continue with it. I also had no choice but to replace my tire with a larger, heavier duty brand. Carol thought this was a good idea anyway, envisioning rough roads ahead.

That fifth of June, as we cycled through more miles of Kansas wheat, we created the Mudd/Golubock Bikers' Law, a mathematical formula for the distance we traveled on our bikes related to the many variables we encountered. In my head, I gathered all the concepts I wanted to reflect, and Carol put them together in a tidy equation: $Y = Dw \times Vw \times G \times Ejc$, where Y is the distance we traveled, Dw is the direction of the wind, Vw is the velocity of the wind, G is the grade, and Ejc is Gibi's and Carol's energy. For me, the latter was as changeable and powerful as the wind. My energy level depended on what kind of mood I was in, how I was feeling about Carol, what my dreams were like the night before, what kind of phone conversation I'd had with Tony, how anxious I was about my bike, and how much or little I was oriented toward "being here now," rather than fifty miles farther east.

It was late by the time we arrived in Hutchinson, smack in the middle of Kansas. The town made me nervous. Hutchinson was larger than most of the towns we'd been in, more urban, more run-down, more kids cruising the streets in souped-up cars. My uneasy feelings were reinforced when a man at the Mexican restaurant where we ate told us two girls had been killed recently not far to the north. After dinner, I dragged Carol to the police station to ask the location of a legal campground. The only one in the area was all the way on the other side of town but we made the trip anyway. I'll never know what my intuition was about, but at least I felt safe that night.

DAY 37: It was one thing to be philosophical about slowing down and another thing to do it and accept it. The next day, we biked another whopping thirty-four miles! The morning road was a patchwork of pot holes, chuck holes and torn-up pavement. I crashed into one of the gashes in the road at high speed, losing my pedals and letting the early morning light between me and my seat. For a moment, I thought it was all over. I damned my eyes which couldn't distinguish shadows from holes until it was too late.

Despite the obstacles, the ride felt good because it was the first morning that Carol was feeling like her old self, and it wasn't long before we'd arrived in Newton, Kansas. The town was full of surprises. In our usual manner, we stripped off as much as possible at the Laundromat, loaded the machines, and left for what we thought would be a quick excursion into town.

First, we hit the local health food store where we warmed our hearts on carob ice cream sandwiches. At Western Auto, we picked out two spiffy rain-proof bike covers; no more jumping out of warm sleeping bags at night and thrashing around with cellophane bike tarps. What a luxury *that* would be! Our next stop was the Coventry Bike Shop where we were received like royal visitors by the friendly and professional shopkeepers. Intending to make only a few minor adjustments, I set Little Silver up on a rack outside in the roasting sun. Four hours later, I had finished cleaning, replacing, and adjusting parts. The time spent with those knowledgeable bike people was totally reassuring and comforting. I left wondering what such unusually competent people were doing in the middle of Kansas.

When we finally got back to the Laundromat, our clothes were gone. Calmly, we searched each machine and dryer. No luck. Was there a dirty-clothes freak in Newton, Kansas? We tried to stay very nonchalant about the whole disaster. We called the managers phone number on the wall, but that person was no longer the manager. In despair, I called Tony. As I was bemoaning our plight, a middle-aged woman walked in, went straight to the back of the building and unlocked the back room. I dropped the phone and Carol leapt out of her chair as the woman brought out our clothes – washed, dried and folded. What bliss! I've never been so grateful for a pile of laundry before or since.

That night we camped at the Girl Scout Park. After eating nutritious food, writing in our journals and cleaning up all our trash, we proceeded to drink a full bottle of wine and a half-pint of Kahlua. It was a record consumption of alcohol, but we were so exhausted we barely noticed. Despite being slightly punchy, we formulated a plan to get to Pittsburg, Kansas, 200 miles away, by Friday to pick up our mail. This was Tuesday night.

DAY 38: Wednesday was the first sunny day we'd had in a long time, and we felt equally bright and cheerful. In the late afternoon a blessed tailwind blew us into a little cafe outside Severy just ahead of black, ominous storm clouds. Two patrol cars were parked outside, and inside, two sheriffs were sipping coffee, smoking, and cracking jokes with the waitress. It was a classic scene from "In the Heat of the Night." We asked if we could pitch our tent behind the cafe. After thoroughly looking us over and carefully considering this unusual occurrence, they agreed it would be okay. Upon further reflection, however, one of the sheriffs suggested that, what with the storm brewing and the cafe's proximity to the busy highway, we'd be better off spending the night behind Sheriff Jones's trailer a mile down the road. The offer sounded safe enough, and, following our resolution to spend more time with local folks, we accepted.

When we stayed at anyone's home, we tried to be as unobtrusive as possible. All we asked was to have water and a place to pitch our tent. On this occasion, we took the liberty of eating our dinner on the Jones lawn chairs. When the Sheriff's wife, Nadine, invited us in for tea and a shower, our day was made.

Their trailer was a tiny, rectangular metal box, jammed tight with a sofa, two chairs, a small coffee table and a big TV set. The kitchen was at one end of the trailer and served as their dining room and sitting area. I went to the other end to take the first bath, leaving Carol to make conversation.

The bath tub was the size of a butter dish, but it was hot, steamy and luxurious. I was appalled by the giant ring of dirt that appeared as the water drained from the tub, and I searched in all the cupboards for cleanser so nobody would see it. When I finally emerged, I found Carol in the middle of Cliff Jones's rock and relic collection—boxes and boxes of flints, arrowheads and crystals, some randomly piled in old shoeboxes, others wrapped painstakingly in individual pieces of tissue in cigar boxes. The Sheriff was immensely proud of his collection, describing where he had gathered them, pulling out special pieces for closer inspection. I *was* interested, but mostly I was enjoying the happy warmth of being in a home. I relished the smells coming from the kitchen, the homey feeling of Cliff in his T-shirt with his slippered feet propped up on the sofa, the iced tea I sipped from a pink plastic glass. Carol went for her turn in the bathroom, and I took a turn at becoming acquainted with Cliff and Nadine.

He talked, she listened and supported him, filling in the details of his stones, gathering materials as he needed them. Besides the flints and rocks, there were guns, bullets and clippings from local newspapers. A movie called "Bad Company" had been filmed in Severy and made hot news for several weeks. Cliff began to talk about his exploits as a sheriff—the high-speed chases, the arrests—describing each in great detail. Carol arrived (after scouring out *her* ring) in time to hear of the Great Dope Bust. A group of farmers had been growing a lush crop of marijuana in the middle of the Kansas wheat. What a bust it had been! The papers were full of the story and there were photos of Cliff standing over piles of marijuana plants, the hunter with his trophy. Carol and I exchanged amused grins as Cliff told his best story.

We sat comfortably on the sofa while they ate their dinner of steak, iceberg salad, white bread and butter. They offered us the use of their small camper truck to sleep in as it was still threatening to storm. Gratefully, we scrunched into the tiny double bed and fell asleep, hoping that *now* the big storm would hit and be gone by morning.

DAY 39: I don't like coffee—never have—but somehow I didn't mind drinking the cup Nadine served me that next morning. We sat at the breakfast table eating our granola while she asked us about our journey. With Cliff gone off to work, we asked her about herself. What was it like to be married to a sheriff? She said she constantly lived with the fear that each night he wouldn't return. Her complete economic and emotional dependence on her husband seemed to us an intolerable situation. How much we valued our own freedom and independence! We left her standing on the stoop of the trailer, watching after us. Would this be the night he wouldn't come home?

As Carol shot off in the lead, I got really angry. I resented her assumption that she should always lead; I, too, wanted the excitement of feeling I was the first one to see whatever there was to see, to be the scout of our party. I loved to pretend I was a pioneer adventuring into unexplored territory. I had watched the back of Carol's three T-shirts until I could count the number of stripes with my eyes closed. Despite my efforts to deny, ignore and overcome my competitive drive, I still wanted to have my share of being first. My biggest problem was that I was chicken to ask Carol to relinquish her monopoly of the lead. Stewing over this dilemma, I biked in silence behind her.

Carol was feeling nauseous that day, and we stopped from time to time so she could drink a soda to settle her upset stomach. During one of those stops, we got into a serious conversation about people assuming their own power—power over their workplaces, over their environment, their lives, their bodies. How easy it is to relinquish that responsibility to others, especially to those willing to take it. The discussion started when Carol told me she felt she was letting me do too much doctoring of her physical ailments. I would suggest she move the Ace bandage a certain way, that she shouldn't bike more than half a day, that she ought to eat certain kinds of food or wear certain clothes. She was all too inclined to go along with my suggestions, but she felt she ought to do more of the doctoring herself. This conversation made me realize that I would have to take responsibility for my own needs and desires. I would have to develop the courage to ask for what I wanted—to feel I had that right—rather than depend upon Carol's perception and sensitivity to provide me with those things.

It took this conversation and the rest of the day for me to muster up the courage for the Big Confrontation (I want the lead!). In my mind I concocted all the possible conversations we might have. They all involved great conflict and disagreement. My fixation told me a lot about my perspective of human relationships and how differences are resolved. If I imagined all disagreement ended in anger, hurt and rejection, no wonder I wanted to avoid conflict at all costs.

At the end of the day we arrived in Girard, Kansas, to discover that the motel the guidebook assured us was there, wasn't. We went to the public pool, swam and showered. The disappointment eased. As we stood in front of the mirror combing out our hair, I said I needed a "criticism/self-criticism time"—that was what we called our confession and sharing times. Carol was immediately worried.

We went outside to dry our hair in the sun and I told her what was bothering me. Expecting a huge scene, I was surprised and relieved when she *agreed* with me that she was being too possessive about the lead and said she'd be more sensitive to my wanting to go first. She was relieved because she thought I was going to complain about her being sick again. I reassured her that I was not the least bit angry about her feeling sick (what could she do about it?), although I was not as sympathetic as I could have been. Since I don't allow myself to be sick or in need, I have a difficult time supporting and giving to others who are. It was a hard conversation, and after it, we felt relieved and close. We resolved that she would not apologize for her physical problems, and I would ask more readily for what I wanted.

We ended the day in a beautiful grove of giant trees in a rest area outside Girard. It was a dark, secretive corner of the world, a place filled with mystery and magic. But all was not well. Carol's stomach was still upset, and she was only able to eat a little fruit and cottage cheese. We both worried about her.

The Ozarks

As they advanced the ground became rougher and hiller.

DAY 40: We made it to Pittsburg, Kansas, on Friday with miles and time to spare. We had a good breakfast at Otto's, the local favorite. The people in Pittsburg gave us one of the warmest welcomes we'd yet had. I had lost an earring in the Jones' trailer in Severy and needed to replace it. The local jeweler, an old grandfatherly type,

treated us as if we were his long-lost grandchildren, calling us "little kids." At first, I was offended and insisted on telling him we were twenty-nine years old. After a while, I began to accept and enjoy the genuine concern and affection he wanted so much to give us. He found a pair of earrings that matched mine, polished one of them and handed it to me as a gift. Not forgetting Carol, he found a little pair of studs and presented them to her with his good wishes for a safe trip.

The owner of the local barber shop, who had kept an eye on our bikes while we had breakfast, asked us to pose for a series of pictures. (Several months later, much to my amazement and delight, he sent me copies of those pictures.) He even called the local newspaper to do a story on us, but we wanted to move on. We picked up our stack of mail from General Delivery at the post office and bid warm and grateful farewells to Kansas.

Just across the Missouri border, in the company of a local farm cat, we read our mail, some to ourselves, some out loud to each other. My friend Gerry had sent a finger puppet for a one-puppet show on a back country road. The first performance, delivered to a small, select audience—Carol, our bikes and the cat—was a welcome to Missouri. "Hi there, Carol and Gibi. Here you are in Missouri. I hear that the hills are *something else!*" We nodded our heads, imagining the ups and downs to come. "But you guys shouldn't have much trouble. You're in great shape, and people in these parts are *real* friendly. Why, just the other day. . . ." We sat under the gnarled, umbrella-shaped tree for a good half hour. I felt a bit homesick as well as excited. The farm cat reminded me of my own gray cat, Frieda. Carol and I took turns "kitty-kittying" it and rubbing its tummy. We had arrived in the Midwest, yet another area as unfamiliar to me as outer space. What would Missouri be like? Who lived here in the middle of the country?

By evening, we'd pedaled fifty-five miles into the new state; an easy ride, not unlike Kansas. At twilight, we left Greenfield with our supply of groceries to look for a place to spend the night. Since our maps showed no rest areas or parks along the route, we decided to try a new approach—camping in farmyards. We'd sure find out who lived in Missouri that way.

Our first prospect was a small, white, box house perched high on a knoll, surrounded by a green lawn and pastures in which grazed a solitary milk cow. From our vantage point on the hill opposite, it looked friendly and inviting. We plunged down the hill to the driveway and wheeled our bikes up to the front door. I knocked, and knocked some more. I could see people sitting in the back room. Why didn't they come to the door? We went around to the side door, having some second thoughts about the idea. I knocked and banged louder. Still no response. I began to get very edgy and unsure of myself. What right did I have to intrude on somebody's private life and ask to spend the night at their house? But the need to collapse for the night *now* made me stick my head in the door and yell, "Anybody home?!" I closed the door quickly, feeling like a Halloween trick-or-treater. We waited.

When the door finally opened, I almost lost my breath. The man who answered was the oldest person I had ever seen in my life. His face had creases and deep wrinkles criss-crossing every which way. I thought I had discovered the oldest man alive. Having had little experience with old people, I wanted to turn right around and ride away. What should I do now? How should I behave? What should I say?

The first thing I learned was that I had to shout. We explained how it was that we had arrived at this house and awkwardly made our request to spend the night. While his eyes told us how incredulous he was, his face wrinkled into a welcoming smile, his delight apparent at this unusual event. With gesturing and enthusiasm, he directed us to a spot on the lawn that would allow us a reasonably level sleep. So far, so good. While we were chopping vegetables, the old man's wife came and stood on the front steps and watched us. Carol went over to say hello. I remembered with a knot growing in my stomach all the times as a child I'd had to visit my grandmother and make polite conversation. When Carol returned, suggesting we visit our hosts, Ches and Minnee Magee, in the morning, I could only fantasize the scene of sitting properly, knees together, hands in my lap, in my lady-like clothes in Granmonnie's library while she scrutinized me. "Don't you think that dress is awfully short, dear?"—her piercing tone betraying the sickly-sweet smile on her cream-shiny face.

DAY 41: Minnee and Ches were *not* like Granmonnie. They invited us in for breakfast; Carol and Ches whipped up fried eggs and toast for everybody. The home-churned butter melting on our toast was as bright yellow-orange as the yolk of a grass-fed chicken's egg. The fresh cream they poured over their Rice Krispies was thick, rich and warm. From time to time throughout the meal, they would remind each other to take their respective medicines.

Minnee and Ches had lived in that box farmhouse for sixty years, ever since they'd married. I marveled at how well they complemented each other in their old age: Ches couldn't hear too clearly, but Minnee's ears were still sharp; Minnee could barely hobble for her painful arthritis and rheumatism, but Ches still got around fine. They lived alone taking care of most of their own needs with the help of their son and his family who lived down the road. I felt for the moment as though I'd stepped into a Grandma Moses painting. While methodically eating her cereal, Minnee asked Ches what he was going to do that day. Ches replied that he'd probably do about the same thing he'd done yesterday. Minnee smiled a knowing smile. "Well, I guess that won't be too much."

After breakfast, Carol collected our gear while I stayed to help Minnee with the dishes. I felt so satisfied, forever content to be standing at that kitchen window with the sun streaming through the curtains, looking out over the pasture where the milk cow grazed, washing dishes in the hot, soapy water, putting the table scraps in the bucket for Ches to take out to the garden. After the dishes were stacked by the sink, she went back to the living room to sit in her chair in front of the furnace. It was already like an oven in the house, but it was the only way to keep her joints loose. I helped her put on her stockings.

She talked about the farm, her children and her life almost as if I weren't there sitting on a little stool at her feet. "Animals, she said, "have to stay in their rightful place. They should be outside." The Magees had no pets. How different my own life was, horses on the front porch, chickens in the house, cats on the kitchen counter, dogs on the bed and couches. Animals had always had more space in my heart than most people. It was only after Annie came that I realized that they walked all over me. I was beginning to glimpse some truth in what Minnee was saying.

I felt as though I'd just found grandparents—at last—and was having to leave before I'd had a chance to get to know them. I was sad about both my empty childhood family life, and the need for a "family" on the road. The romance of camping out was wearing down and I longed to have *one* resting place. Unexpected tears came to my eyes as we rolled our bikes down the driveway. Since the Magees driveway ended at the bottom of a hill, our cold bodies, stiff knees and teary eyes got a good jolt as we strained up the grade.

We were on the famous Missouri roller coaster for fifty-five miles that day, one hill after another. Pedal slowly up one hill in low gear—not too bad until the very top—crest the hill, shift gradually into high gear, zoom down the other side. In the valley between hills, quickly shift into low gear again—one, two, three, four, five-pump hard, crest. Shift, zoom, pedal, shift . . . forever and ever. It was one of the most physically strenuous days I can remember.

A family in a sedan pulled up alongside of me to find out just what we were doing. While shifting, pumping, cresting, zooming, I told them our story. They were incredulous. As they slowly pulled back, I began to gear up for a steep hill ahead. Thinking I'd *really* impress them, I burst forth up the hill with great speed. Twang! A small muscle in my right calf gave a sharp, wrenching pain. For the rest of the day, I had to figure out some way to avoid putting pressure on that leg, and even now, when I try to push too hard, the little calf muscle squeaks to be remembered. "Don't try to impress anyone, stupid; just make it in one piece." I call it my humility muscle.

Exhausted, we rolled over an interstate (our first since Las Vegas) into Marshfield in mid-afternoon. I was suddenly struck with a hay fever attack. I couldn't stop sneezing and my eyes itched and swelled, my nose ran profusely. The paved highway and speeding travelers shook us abruptly from our quiet world of back country roads. Along with the interstate, went all the trappings and trimmings—giant supermarkets, fast food joints and myriad gas stations.

Despite our aversion to such concentrated commercialism, we were pleased to find a giant food store which offered us a selection of produce that we couldn't find in remote rural areas. However, the farther east we went, the more frequently the produce was packaged and standardized, wrapped and sealed in plastic, always in amounts useless to two people. After fuming and complaining to ourselves a good deal, we finally decided we had a right to ask that the produce be unwrapped and distributed to us in smaller quantities. On our test run, a store clerk begrudgingly unwrapped a bunch of bananas for us. After that, we never again bought more than we wanted; tomatoes would be disengaged from their cellophane tubes, peaches freed from their Styrofoam trays, bananas released from their bond of stretchy green tape.

I was still in the throes of the hay fever attack when we left the asphalt city. After several miles, we started our nightly search for a campsite. We were disappointed when a house on a green lawn hill turned out to be deserted. We kept going. Eventually, we knocked on the door of a modern, well-to-do looking farmhouse. After recovering from her surprise at our presence and request, the woman of the house directed us to the lawn in front of an abandoned Victorian nearby. The old house had obviously been out-classed by the new ranch-style house. Around us were newly-painted equipment sheds and two huge dairy barns, the kind you see on calendars sent by insurance companies. I went to investigate the barn nearby on the pretense of looking for water. Inside, milk was being mechanically pumped from cows' udders into a stainless steel tank. The continual drone of the machine and pumps drowned out the soft sounds of cows lowing and munching hay, the farmhand occasionally cursing, reprimanding or cajoling the animals.

As soon as I saw the raggedy old farm dog, I knew I was in for a hard night. She was a mangy combination of collie, German shepherd and beagle. She carried as many pests with her as breeds—ringworm, gnats, fleas, lice and ticks. She could not move more than a few feet without suddenly sitting down and scratching violently. I might have believed she was going crazy except I knew she must have had this condition for most of her life and somehow survived it. She was a sweet dog, overjoyed with the attention we gave her. Once we discovered the condition of her health, however, we tried to discourage her company. Sensing our aversion to her, she tried not to beg for attention, but found our love and care—however reserved—irresistible. She stayed on her favorite chair on the porch of the old house for most of the evening, occasionally venturing down to visit us, wagging and scratching, always with a swarm of creatures around her.

I had scouted around in the old house and discovered a mattress, much to my delight, for I was ready for a change in sleeping arrangements. I dragged it onto the porch, fitted it out with a piece of old curtain and lay down my sleeping bag. There was even a pillow. Carol had set the tent up on the lawn and thought my idea of sleeping in the abandoned place was crazy—it gave her the creeps and she was sure I'd be bitten by some creature before the night was out.

Ghosts and bites were no problem. But midway through the night, the dog with her accompanying entourage of bugs sidled up to the head of the mattress and lay down in front of my face. I tried to ignore her at first, but soon realized I couldn't sleep with this dog and her bugs, no matter how soft my heart was. I coaxed her into a room in the house, fixed a bed with old material and curtains and told her to stay. She was content for a while, but was soon back by my head. (Why do dogs always know where the soft touch is?!) As I stood up to move her somewhere—anywhere—she moved herself right onto the middle of my sleeping bag.

She refused to move no matter how firm or gently persuasive I was. I was on the verge of tears, not knowing what to do with this dog who only wanted a little love and affection. I could easily have given it, but I didn't want my sleeping bag infested with insects for the rest of the trip. (What had Minnee Magee said about putting animals in their places?) Gritting my teeth, I shoved and kicked her with my foot (I didn't even want to touch her). I had *never* kicked an animal in my life. My proddings didn't bother her a bit—she was used to that kind of treatment no doubt. But with every kick, I tortured myself. She finally caught on that I *really* didn't want her around and slinked off into the night. My misery was absolute. In shock, I reached down deep in my bag and pulled out "Puppy," my little stuffed puppet dog, a childhood friend that I'd brought with me, and cried myself to sleep.

DAY 42: The weather next morning was as muggy and congested as I was. On top of my hay fever, my shattered self-image of a kind person brought more tears as I told Carol my story. Despite feeling poorly again herself, she listened and comforted me.

We started off, in our own private worlds of heartache and stomachache, Carol in the lead. After some time, wanting to prove to her and to myself that I could keep up a good pace even on the roller coaster, I pulled forward to pass. As I was overtaking her, she said she felt we ought to each bike at our own pace. I was agreeable to that, although confused as to why she needed to say it, and pulled ahead. At that point she said she wanted to slipstream; that is, to use the windbreak of the lead bike to pull the second one along. I translated that to mean that as long as she was in the lead, "our own paces" was the way to go; but when she was behind, that wasn't acceptable. I was irritated and snapped, "I think you just don't want me to be in the lead." When she confessed to feeling quite nauseous, I felt more understanding. We rode close together for the rest of the afternoon.

As we pedaled our sweaty ailing bodies over one hill that hot afternoon, we were hailed by two bike tourists standing on the far side of the road. Had we heard of "Lazy Louie"? the woman wanted to know. We hadn't. We found out Lazy Louie runs a "bike camp" for bike tourists which offers a shed with cots and stove, a shower, refrigerator full of beer and spring water, and home-style entertainment. We decided to stop by.

Louie was a paunchy, middle-aged man, full of beer, energy, guitar-singing and talk. He seemed lonely, and it obviously gave him pleasure to provide a "home" for cyclists on their various cross-country journeys. That particular day, his continual chatter and our moods fit together like a pickle with ice cream, so we stayed just long enough for some cold spring water, a song, and signing his guest book.

We continued on through the muggy air. It was a strange area. Turtles the size of hamburgers littered the road, some living, some smashed—pieces of hard, brittle shell stuck to exposed soft underbellies. There was something of me in each of those helpless turtles so far out of their element. When we stopped at Piney River for a dip, we found the shore littered with fish heads. The whole scene was revolting and the place stank, but we desperately needed a swim.

I came across a little pool of captured pollywogs. Here was my chance to be kind to animals again! I carefully freed the captives, shooing them out into the river. As we turned to leave, I happened to look back to the river. A little boy was carefully rebuilding his water dam, herding more pollywogs into his camp. I apologized to him for ruining his work. He stared blankly at me while I explained about animals needing to be free. I left feeling awful.

We treated ourselves to a motel that night in Houston, Missouri, the first in several days. My crotch had developed small rubbing sores from not bathing and applying healing salve frequently enough. My whole body felt withered and dried out; it absorbed cream like a sponge. We soaked up the hot shower and the cool, air-conditioned room. New bodies, clean clothes. Now we were ready for the *really* steep Missouri hills.

DAY 43: Compared to the Ozark walls that rose up before us, the Rockies seemed like sand dunes. Neither of us had ever worked harder getting over any grade before. We were frustrated and humiliated and only partially compensated for our struggle by the spectacular country. This was the river recreation area of Missouri. Clean rivers flowed through lush, heavily-forested mountains. In Alley Springs, we stopped for a short swim in water so clear we were momentarily lifted from our low spirits. Only later did we find out that we could have rented a canoe and paddled down-river, sent our bikes ahead in a truck, and avoided many miles of torturous hill-climbing.

Anxious to be done with the worst of the hills, we set off immediately after lunch. I pulled ahead of Carol, feeling rejuvenated. The water had washed away the hay fever, the trauma with the old dog, and the bitter memory of my "lost grandparents." Since I had a slightly lower gear than Carol, I was able to move more steadily up the grades. In the middle of one that was particularly steep, I heard a choking noise behind me. It sounded like Carol was gagging on something. I looked back and was startled to realize she was crying. She was struggling up the hill, and finally stopped. She had eaten little for the past five days. Now, the sounds of frustration and humiliation at her weakness and sickness came from deep within. I was relieved that I was not the only one to cry on the trip, and eager to comfort her.

We stopped at the top of the hill and sat at the edge of the road, looking into the forest. I was wrapped in my own strong emotions; feeling awkward and embarrassed by her weakness, yet also feeling a strong concern and love for her. She was quick to recover her composure but still felt low and discouraged. She wouldn't hear of hitching. So we biked up, over and down a few more hills until we reached the public campground at Owls Bend.

It was an expansive park with picnic tables, fire places, outhouses and campsites, situated alongside the same swiftly moving river we'd swum in eighteen miles back at Alley Springs. After setting up camp, we splashed and floated in the cool water, drifting downstream, walking back up, drifting down, over and over. We felt alive and happy again, except for Carol's nagging nausea. I knew she was greatly minimizing the extent of the sickness. We tried to trace it back. Where had we been? What had we eaten? The only suspect was the old dried skim milk on top of tired-out granola, although it wasn't reasonable that so little of a food she'd been eating for so long could cause such a problem now.

That evening as we talked about the problem, we touched on the possibility that she might have "morning sickness." She'd been with Arthur two and a half months earlier. But it was an unlikely and unthinkable explanation, particularly because—like me—she'd not had a menstrual period for nearly three years. The possibility of pregnancy was too heavy a subject to spend much time speculating about, but we did resolve to consult a doctor as soon as possible. We couldn't continue the trip at the rate we were going with Carol's condition. We went to sleep with worried thoughts—accompanied by heavy snoring from the camp area next to us.

DAY 44: The morning presented us with a couple of monstrous hills and two new adventures in adversity—"Loose Gravel" and "Fresh Oil." A county road worker, sensing our dismay commiserated with us about the hills. Each time he passed us that morning—hauling loads of loose gravel and fresh oil—he gave us a sympathetic and encouraging wave.

We finally arrived, a few hills walked up, in Ellington where we found an open health clinic. The doctor was immediately available. He was a stocky older man with gray hair and wire-rimmed spectacles; but his image of the companionable country doctor was not matched by his conduct. He was singularly unhelpful and not particularly friendly. He had no advice or ideas on why Carol was having stomach trouble, asked few questions and gave an inept, uncaring impression. We finally suggested he run a pregnancy test; it didn't seem to have occurred to him. He returned with the result and—I thought—a glint in his eye to report that Carol was indeed pregnant. He seemed to take a sadistic pleasure in delivering information that would cause such grief, confusion and problems in our lives.

We managed to get out of the office before the wave of disbelief and horror overcame Carol. There was so much to deal with; the unwanted, unexpected pregnancy, the need for a decision, the fear of considering abortion, of having to tell Arthur, the possibility of ending the trip, of going home (!), the uncertainty of how her family and friends would handle the news, the strange and inhospitable surroundings.

I urged her to call her best friend, Stephanie, in San Francisco, knowing it would help. Meanwhile, I sat across the street in the shade, trying to understand how I fit into this sea of troubles. The possibility of pregnancy had seemed so remote that the reality which had been dealt us with such lack of compassion was that much more unbelievable and shattering.

We checked into a motel, attracted by pool-side rooms—and were led to a drab cubicle on the underside of the complex The darkness added another level to the depression we were fast sinking into. While I went shopping in town, I called Tony to tell him what was happening. I told him we might end the trip because Carol would probably have to spend some time in the hospital (although she was still undecided about an abortion), or she would be going home since she couldn't finish the trip weighing 105 pounds and not eating. After all, we still had a few mountains to go over and coal country to go through. I watched a growing excitement rising in me about going *home*. After six weeks on the road, home looked very appealing again, and I found myself longing for its comforts and security. Tony was calm and unemotional. Later, I learned that he had joyfully gone around his office telling everyone that I was coming home.

For the rest of that day, June thirteenth, Carol was on the phone to Arthur, Stephanie, and her older brother, Harvey. As the day progressed, she became more calm and decisive. She wanted to have another test done, to have another consultation, and then to have the quickest abortion possible. In Washington, D.C., Arthur was getting information on clinics, doctors and methods. He was helpful and sensitive, despite what I imagined was a terrible shock for him as well. Carol made an appointment at the only abortion clinic in the state, in St. Louis, and we decided to hitch the 160 miles north to get there. By this time, there was little question in our minds that she was pregnant. It was just a matter of finding out how far along she was and whether she had found out early enough to have the vacuum process.

We talked that night about how this affected our plans. If she could have the abortion and be back on her feet within a couple of days, we could finish the trip. Oddly enough, however, I wasn't upset at the thought of our trip ending at the Mississippi River instead of at the Atlantic Ocean. Somehow, the goal wasn't as important as it had been before.

We went to bed with a total sense of uncertainty. It was the first time on our trip that we had not been in control of our journey. We had to find out certain things which only professional people could tell us; this left us feeling dependent, lost and helpless. This sudden turn of events impressed on me the need to live each day to the fullest.

DAY 45: Our trip to St. Louis was pleasant enough under the circumstances. I hadn't hitched more than once before in my life so the idea of hitching 160 miles was a source of considerable anticipation and excitement. Our first ride was with an old hay baler who operated a small farm with his sons. After he left us off ten miles up the road, we decided to bike for awhile because it was such an exquisite day. But we didn't go very far; a pregnant woman shouldn't do too much serious biking.

Our next short truck ride brought us close to a major intersection where we could pick up a ride to the interstate, and from there to St. Louis. Dwayne fit perfectly into our scheme. He was a construction foreman who traveled around the state, supervising jobs. In fact, he'd been the foreman on the Hub City Motel where we'd spent the last horrible day and night. He was a quiet, family man, pleasant and easy to ride with. He loved Missouri—been born and raised there—and pointed out things of interest as we drove along. Our senses were overloaded, riding along at such great speed without putting in any effort at all. The miracle of motor travel!

Dwayne left us at a gas station on the interstate to St. Louis. As we sat on the block wall outside the station, a VW bus pulled in for gas, the van door jerked open and two small boys made a dash for the restrooms. After chatting a few minutes with their father, we decided to ask if he could take us into St. Louis. He was happy to help, so we dismantled our bikes and gear and shoved it all into the space at the back of the bus. The two boys and their tiny kitten were on their way to the big city to visit their grandparents for the weekend. We were pleased to be part of their company—until the father told us he had to stop at the state mental hospital to pick up his wife. Why, I wondered, did there always have to be some hitch, some new challenge to cope with? I fell silent, contemplating the man's "crazy" wife in the car with us for two hours. When I saw the woman in white uniform walk briskly to the car and kiss her husband hello, I almost let out of loud sigh of relief. She was full of stories about her classes in student nursing.

We were overwhelmed by the city; the interstate, crisscrossing freeways, towering buildings, the vast stretches of urban sprawl. I felt like a combination of country bumpkin and refugee. When the family dropped us off in the neighborhood of the clinic, we set about searching for a suitable motel. The first couple of prospects were filled, and the third was a fancy downtown hotel whose receptionist didn't know whether to call the police or throw us out himself. We finally found a room at the Bel Air Motel. When asked if we had luggage, we replied, "Yes, right outside," and managed, despite our giggles, to wheel our bikes with some dignity through the lobby to our rooms.

Carol was holding up pretty well. I felt extremely protective of her and took pleasure from being able to give her counsel and solace. Her appointment was scheduled for the next day. To take our minds off it, we took a ride on our unpacked bicycles, wildly weaving and zipping like speedsters through the traffic. An excellent fish dinner at an elegant restaurant was marred only by the anxieties that we shared.

Carol and I were so close at this point that whatever emotion or pain was felt by one was shared by the other. It had become *our* pregnancy and *our* abortion. At times I could not differentiate between us and was totally caught up in the drama. I was devoted and committed to taking care of Carol and making sure she received the best possible care. I'd never had such strong feelings before for *anyone.*

DAY 46: Before the appointment at the clinic, Carol talked on the phone for at least an hour to Harvey, Stephanie and Arthur. They called often and had even made plans to come to St. Louis to be with her. Carol was moved by how deeply committed her friends were, by how much they cared and were concerned. It was during those long, continual morning phone calls that I began to feel tight inside and teary. Eventually, I recognized that I was envious and jealous of all the attention she was getting and needed some support myself. I was embarrassed by my own needs and only reluctantly shared them with her. At her suggestion and encouragement, I resolved to call a few of my own close friends when I had a good chance to do so.

To kill time, we took another short ride in the park, pedaling until the appointed hour. It was a relief to finally arrive at the abortion clinic. The staff there was wonderful, as thoughtful and understanding of my situation as they were of Carol's. I was impressed that they offered a counseling session for family and friends of the abortion client, to inform them of procedures and what they could do to make the trauma easier.

Carol disappeared into the office and I went downstairs to make phone calls. First, I spoke to Paula and a couple of the teachers at the pre-school. They were very sympathetic and said how much they missed me and wanted me to come home. It was the worst thing I could have heard. How much I *wanted* to go home! It would be a glorious return: getting off the airplane into Tony's open arms; maybe a few close friends would be waving and smiling, happy to see me; walking through the front door to a grand reception by the dogs and cats; maybe a surprise welcome-home party. The fantasies made me warm and happy. I felt I was losing my grip on my resolve to remain calm, flexible and open to any course of action. It was still entirely possible that we could go on; I'd had more than a passing feeling that Carol might not be pregnant at all—even as she sat upstairs in the clinic—but I hadn't shared that with her. She hadn't needed more doubt and uncertainty.

Next I called an older special friend who worked in a public-interest organization. My call found Sally in the middle of a meeting and the secretary said she could not interrupt her. I almost gave in, defeated, then found myself saying to the woman on the phone that I *had to* speak with her, that it was extremely important and would she please let Sally know who was on the phone. My courage and persistence amazed me. Not only did Sally come on the line, but she was not at all angry at being interrupted. We talked about abortion and how deeply she felt it touched women.

The sound of her voice, her wisdom, calmness and understanding soothed me. Her parting words were to call *any* time I needed her.

My sister wasn't home, but by that time I was tired and went back upstairs to wait for Carol. When she came out of the office, the look on her face told me everything. She wasn't pregnant. We left the office in a daze, both of us relieved but shocked by this sudden change of events. The agony, the hurt, the despair we'd been through because we believed she was carrying a child—it had all been so unnecessary.

A couple of blocks from the clinic it hit me. I had no excuse to go home anymore; there was no hope of returning to the security I longed for. Bursting into tears, I collapsed on a patch of lawn, miserably aware that people passing by and people in cars stopped at the light were staring at me. I cried for what I'd been through, for trying so hard to remain objective but not succeeding, for wanting to go home and knowing I couldn't. Now Carol was the strong one. She was completely understanding and sympathetic, and I believe she would have given up the rest of the trip for me if I truly had been unwilling to go on. But she said she thought we could pick ourselves up and get back on the road again, finish our journey together, our lives closer and richer for the experience we'd come through. In my heart I knew she was right, that I should go on, and that I'd feel better about myself if I didn't give up now. It took a bit of doing, a bit of gentle prodding, but slowly I got into the spirit again. I was touched by how much Carol cared about me. I was as important to her as she was to me.

So we began to gear up again. First there were phone calls to some very surprised people. False alarm. Arthur, of course, was greatly relieved. Tony didn't let on how disappointed he was that I wasn't coming home He bolstered me up and sent us off with all his good wishes. A horrible ordeal, a bad dream was coming to an end. What else was in store for us? What dramas would unfold at the top of the next hill?

To relax and unwind, we went to see the film, "Unmarried Woman" which rekindled our faith in what we were doing. We found a fine natural foods restaurant and had a supper of salad and Haagen Daz ice cream. I was definitely glutted by the over-consumption of good food and looked forward to getting back to our road routine again.

DAY 47: Friday morning we spent shopping for a few essentials and replacing Little Silver's bottom bracket at a bike store. At the tail end of rush hour on Friday afternoon, we moved out into the blaring, bustling traffic and slowly made our way to the edge of the city amidst honking and hooting and belching automobiles. We were forced by heavy traffic to hitch a ride over the Mississippi River—an added insult. We stopped outside Waterloo, Illinois, twenty-five miles from St. Louis, gritty and wired. We spent the night in the backyard of a suspicious old couple, in the company of their 14-year-old, blind but not mute dog, Pepper, and an outhouse covered with pink roses. Carol hadn't been nauseous since the day of her appointment at the abortion clinic.

DAY 48: With the crossing of a new state border, the images and the intensity of the four previous days began to fade, although there still remained a bittersweet taste and a confused anger that the incident had happened at all. We were ready to move on, to really make miles after struggling along so slowly through Kansas and Missouri. However, that first morning in Illinois, Carol came up with two flat tires within a half hour, and the headwind was blowing like a jet stream. After the second tube change, Carols bottom bracket began to develop disturbing clicking noises that grew increasingly worse. Knowing that a faulty bottom bracket is a serious problem, we decided to try to hitch to the nearest bike store in Carbondale before it closed. We couldn't stand the thought of sitting around for the weekend until the stores opened on Monday.

We managed cycling forty miles to Sparta. With our bikes lying forlornly on the sidewalk, Carol and I took turns trying to enlist a sympathetic pickup truck in 100 degree weather. Life was throwing us a bunch of rotten eggs. We'd had our share—*we* thought—of slowdowns, misfortune, flat tires and headwinds, and we figured we were due for a change. After too many hot minutes, we made a sign: "Broken Bikes: Carbondale or Route 51!" It worked. One pickup truck took us nineteen miles to Pinckneyville, and we waited there no more than ten minutes. Our second ride came from a young local coal miner named Chuck, who called in late for work so he could take us the thirty miles to Carbondale. We arrived with plenty of time for bike repairs and a leisurely evening in a local motel.

DAY 49: The next day—Father's Day—started out hot and muggy amidst rolling hills and lush bottomlands. We and our bikes felt good and I knew it would be a good day. My faith was momentarily shaken when—Crash! Bump . . . bump . . . bump. We'd hit a pot-holed, chewed-up back road. Sigh. Taking things as they came, not getting wrapped up in expectations seemed impossible to learn; still does. But after a few miles, the road smoothed out again and so did the day. We were even blessed by a stiff tailwind in the late afternoon as we raced toward the Ohio River and the Kentucky border.

We stopped just before the bridge at a cafe in Shawneetown to make Father's Day calls. I had been looking forward to calling Dad because I knew it would make him happy, and I wanted to share with him my excitement about our good progress that day. We talked for half an hour, probably our longest phone conversation ever. He was curious and interested in all our tales, and his obvious pride in me made me feel wonderful.

I was pretty proud of myself that afternoon as we crossed the Ohio River. It was particularly exciting since we had missed the chance to cross the "real" river, the Mississippi. As we left the toll plaza on the Kentucky side, we felt as if we were entering a new land, a new time; our fortunes would surely turn good.

Despite our high hopes and excitement, we were acutely aware that some very large black storm clouds were moving swiftly along behind us. We hustled along SR 56 to find a place to spend the night. We'd just managed to put up our tent, finish dinner and visit briefly with the young couple who were our hosts for the night when the storm broke with great deluges of water, thunder and lightning. It was the kind of storm I love to watch from inside a cozy house on an overstuffed couch next to a big picture window.

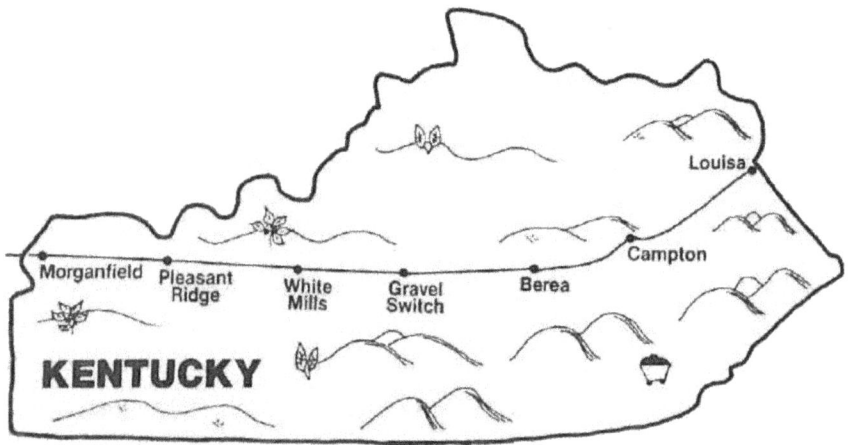

The East

The country here is rich and pleasant, but you must pass through rough and dangerous places before you reach the end of you journey.

DAY 50: Romantic Kentucky images—bluegrass (was it really blue? I wondered), white running fences, grazing thoroughbreds flicking flies, gamboling foals, stately mansions—soon gave way to Kentucky reality—poverty, soot-caked facades on buildings and people, coal sweat, muggy, gritty air, and grimy, drunken towns. Our first Kentucky town, Sebree, had that peculiar depressing atmosphere so

characteristic of older Eastern cities. The buildings were old and coal-dark brick, fronted by wooden boardwalks. The train tracks crossed through the center of town, leading to and from the coal mines. Old buildings with paneless windows lined the streets; old, unshaven men with toothless smiles lined their porches. Their eyes and faces told a story of hard labor with little return. As we shopped, the old men hung around Carol and me like moths attracted to light. We left as quickly as possible, but the heavy feelings hung on us. Biking through the countryside of beautiful, rolling hills was not enough to erase the bleakness of those towns.

We were so low by lunchtime we decided that we had to look in earnest for some way to treat ourselves. But the pickings in the way of food were so meager that we ended up with a can of sauerkraut and a can of beans in our packs as we left Pleasant Ridge to look for our night's lodging. It was by far our most dismal-looking dinner yet. For the first time, I seriously began to consider opening Gerry's box.

We stopped at a two-story suburban-type house to ask permission to spend the night, and a friendly young man who was just leaving directed us to the back of the house to set up our camp. As we finished spreading out our damp gear over most of the lawn to dry, the lady of the house came to visit.

We talked with Linda Wilson for some time; she took us on a tour of the family's vegetable garden and tobacco fields where her mother-in-law and husband were tending the small tobacco plants. Their youngest son, Travis, seven years old, was enchanted with our adventure and helped us set up our tent and roll out our sleeping bags. He even invited us to his secret clubhouse.

We were feeling more and more like part of the family, and Linda asked if we would share their dinner with them. We were delighted to be saved from sauerkraut and beans, and honored and pleased by the first dinner invitation of our journey. It didn't matter that they had steak, that the green beans were soggy or that me salad was made with iceberg lettuce. When they sat down at the table and said grace, we were part of their prayers. They thanked God for our visit and blessed us for a safe journey onwards. That was good enough. However, we didn't decline any of the banana bread birthday cake Linda had baked for her birthday the next day. We were surprised that she was just our age; years of illness made her look well beyond her thirty years. She and her husband Charlie had been married for fifteen years; they were content and at ease with each other, and we delayed saying goodnight until our eyes would barely stay open.

DAY 51: We were slow to leave in the morning. Linda had made iced tea for us, and we lingered over the breakfast table, enjoying each other's company. As we prepared to leave, she said she would pray for our safety. Somehow, as unreligious as I thought I was, I knew she meant it and that it would help. Being with the Wilson's had given us energy and courage to go on. We hugged and bid teary goodbyes. We waved to Linda until we could no longer see her white housecoat billowing in the doorway.

Despite the warmth and encouragement we'd received at the Wilson's, our Kentucky blues continued on through another sultry day as we rode through lush deciduous forests. Part of our problem was that when we crossed the border into Kentucky, we had felt as if we were "nearly there"—to the East Coast and our final destination, Washington, DC. In fact, even though we'd arrived East, we were still 780 miles from Washington—far from "nearly there." We were finding it hard to regenerate since St. Louis, and after seven weeks on the road, we felt ready to stop. So in this mood, we kept a sharp eye out for treats and incentives to buoy us up: a special dinner, special people, a refreshing swim, a good bottle of wine, a liqueur, a fancy motel, a movie—and there was still Gerry's box . . . . Today, our treat would be a swim in the dam at the Rough River Recreation Area. Imagining torrential Whitewater pouring into the dam, we were amused when we crossed over the "Falls of Rough" which were all of three feet high.

By mid-morning I was really lagging. Having made a last-chance resolution to lose a lot of weight, I had set off with no more than a handful of granola in my stomach. I had been used to eating inordinate amounts of food, particularly in the evening when my stomach turned into a bottomless pit. By the time I'd finished writing in my journal, I'd usually managed to down a half-bag of dried prunes. I wasn't gaining any weight, but I wasn't losing it either. In my usual, compulsive style, I had decided not to eat. Carol gently reminded me that it was ridiculous to bike seventy-five miles a day on no food and tried to reason with me to cut down rather than stop eating. I grumbled but knew she was right. We biked on, headed for swim and lunch at the dam.

Within a few miles of the dam, we realized for the first time that a fierce storm was moving in swiftly behind us. Using my last reserves of energy, we raced to outrun the rain. After an initial wrong turn, we just reached the cover of the bath house when the storm broke. Rain poured on the recreation area in sheets—and we hadn't been under that shelter for more than thirty seconds! We could hardly believe our good fortune as we sat and watched vacationers on the beach gathering up half-eaten picnics, wet towels and children and crowding under the scanty cover of the bath house. Little Silver and Big Blue were soon surrounded by half-naked, dripping bodies. The storm passed through like a locomotive—in and out with great crashings of thunder and streaks of lightning. The sun came out, everyone hurried to claim space on the soggy lawn and wet beach front.

The water was extremely refreshing and pleasant, but the lifeguard was an ass. A limit rope was stretched an absurdly short distance from the shore, and when Carol ducked underneath, she was rudely hailed by bullhorn to get immediately back inside the swimming area. Pig, we thought irritably, and left the water to eat our lunch.

The afternoon was clear and sunny, the biking mellow until, on the recommendation of the Bikecentennial route map, we turned onto a relatively unmarked back road. Soon it turned into gravel, pot holes, a very steep downhill and its uphill counterpart. I was incredulous—and furious. I couldn't believe they would officially recommend such a terrible road. I forced myself not to overlook the lovely natural features that surrounded me—beauty that can only be found on such horrendous roads. It was a tree-shaded, jungle-like environment that formed a passageway down the grade to a small creek. The moisture from the abundant plant life provided natural air-conditioning; it was really very special. In spite of this, I was absorbed by anger, outraged at the discomfort the road was inflicting on me and Little Silver. No longer able to contain myself, I dismounted, found a branch, and beat and cursed invisible Bikecentennial route-makers for all I was worth. I passed the rest of the day in a pleasant and peaceful mood.

We spent the night behind the local grocery store in White Mills, Kentucky, where we discovered corn relish. We hadn't sampled anything like it before, mainly because we were strict about minimizing our refined sugar intake. Compulsive, fanatical label-readers, we selected our food with the pickiness of scratching hens. Besides, reading material was rarely a part of our routine, so we devoured each label with great relish. This time we decided to indulge. We spent a calm evening—and went to sleep directly under a glaring, buzzing fluorescent street light.

DAY 52: I woke up feeling hostile and belligerent towards Carol. I glowered with dislike. I determinedly took the lead and kept a good distance between us. We breakfasted in silence at an interstate truck stop. Fighting off the fury I was feeling, I told her I was in a rotten mood and didn't know why. I decided not to worry about it too much, to just accept it. For the time being, it was enough to have shared the feeling, knowing if the anger surfaced, we could deal with it.

I felt as if hard days were coming at me like bowling balls, knocking down emotional blocks, shattering images. The pain and struggle took different forms, but were almost always centered in my mind or in my heart rather than in my body as some physical ailment. The intensity of the pain and the depth of self-discovery depended on my vulnerability at a particular moment and the specific incident triggering the crisis. Certain things have always hit harder than others. Animals invariably hit the king pin.

When I was younger, I used to cry about every dead animal I saw on the highway. The gentle creatures were so much a part of my life, so much a comfort to me, that I personally felt the loss of each hare, each skunk, each red squirrel that lay flattened on the road. I would remain depressed for several hours after passing the dead animal.

One day on my way to Berkeley to see Linne, I passed a lone German shepherd wandering slowly up the on-ramp to the freeway. I was overcome with grief for the lonely, helpless creature which was unknowingly walking to its death. By the time I arrived at her office, I was sobbing about being unable to rescue the poor dog When Linne asked me what I was doing to save myself, I began to understand how much I identified with lost animals, how much I saw myself as a wandering, lost, lonely soul, wandering up the freeway ramps of my own confused life.

Shortly after leaving the truck stop, Carol and I passed a small, beagle-type puppy on the road. As he ran hopefully after us, tongue lolling, tail wagging, my lost dog drama took hold. For a while, I managed to cry *and* ride my bike. But this was the king pin—lights were flashing and bells were ringing. By the time we arrived in Hodgenville, at Lincoln's birthplace, I ran for the ladies' room in tears. As usual, Carol was there to console me. I washed my face and we wandered around the National Monument for a short time. I was struck by Lincoln's words engraved on the wall of the monument: "I was born, and have ever remained, in the humblest walks of life . . . ." Not only did I feel humble, but my spirits were sinking like the Titanic; I couldn't seem to plug up the holes as they broke. The lost dog trauma was only a small incident. Mostly I felt unbearably tired of the trip.

Carol was feeling pretty low herself that morning, so we stopped early for lunch underneath a magnificent old tree in Howardstown. We felt small and low next to that grand tree. It was time for Gerry's box. I don't know what I expected or hoped to find (a magic, instant remedy for blues? a quick end to the trip?), but I unpacked the box with solemn care. I only knew that from that box came a glimmer of hope, a promise that all was not lost, that somebody cared and understood these blues of ours. I recalled Gerry's mysterious comment to me when he delivered the box—that some of the contents were meant to be left behind. This all became clear as I unwrapped two tiny packets of pansy seeds and soil which we ceremoniously planted under the great tree, watering the new seeds from our water bottles. We each chewed a piece of the gum, I tied the many-colored yarn tassel to my front pack and presented the miniature bouquet of straw flowers to Carol. The dime for a phone call, the stick of incense and the bag of peppermint tea I packed away for the evening. As I chewed the last piece of Dentyne, I knew that my despair was only a passing storm, that the sun would surely come out again.

It was a long storm, however. I began to develop painful saddle-sores. My whole body and spirit remained sweaty, dirty and low. I was counting on the luxury of a shower and bed that night, but when we arrived in Lebanon, there was no motel, only an abundance of liquor stores. We'd finally hit a "wet county" and evidence of it was all around in the dejected, drunken souls who inhabited the bars and liquor stores. Not one person reflected the least glimmer of joy or hope. After much consternation about what I wanted to do—it was I who was so desperate to stay in that night—I decided we ought to leave town as soon as possible. I took a sponge bath at a gas station and changed clothes. We bought a bottle of white wine and set out for the next town to buy some ice before stopping for the night.

The only ice in town came in ten pound bags; we were not deterred—and even managed to be a little entertained by the sight of the ten pound bag of ice strapped to the load on Little Silver's rear. We lumbered out of town to find a suitable farmhouse. It was to be one of our most memorable nights.

The place we picked out looked idyllic: a large, square house situated amongst old trees, high on top of a hill over-looking the fields of mowed hay below. We could see the farmer at work with his crew on the hay baler as we pushed our bikes up the long drive. I knocked at the door, and when there was no response, I banged more loudly, insistently, and was more than slightly embarrassed when an elderly woman walked slowly to the door. She smiled at my embarrassment. She said we would have to ask her brother if we could spend the night, so we walked out to the fields. Even though the sun was low in the sky, the air was muggy and hot, and the dry stubble crackled under our feet as if it would burst into flames. After considering our strange request, the farmer said he guessed it'd be all right if we stayed the night.

We didn't even bother putting the tent up before uncorking our wine bottle and chipping out some ice cubes from our now solid block of ice. The wine was absolutely flat—tasteless—but we drank it with pleasure. As we sat under the trees admiring the view and feeling the soft cool lawn underneath us, a few of the farmhands came to keep us company. Two of the teenagers were particularly curious about our travels. They sounded restless and eager to leave the small Kentucky community they'd lived in since birth. One fellow mentioned that Sam, the old farmer, had a loft in his barn that would make an ideal place to sleep. We agreed and he went to ask about it. He didn't return for some time, and we'd forgotten the idea by the time he came back to say that Sam would speak to us about it later. At sundown, Sam and his sister asked us in for tea.

We were always honored to be invited into peoples' houses. The portraits on the wall, the furniture, the food boxes in the pantry, the knick-knacks on the dining room table told a story that could not be seen from the road. Sam's family's house was simple and very, very old. It appeared that he and his sister lived only in two or three rooms of the large house. There had been five children in the family; the others had married and moved away. Sam and his sister had stayed to take care of their parents and, when they died, the farm. Their story was one of constant labor for economic survival, the loss of the family, a fire which burned most of the house which had to be rebuilt. They were not a happy pair. Their faces reflected the toil on the farm, the hours spent in a clothing factory to scrape money together to pay the mortgage. We sat in the kitchen and then in the plain dining room, drinking tea and watching a fuzzy picture on the television.

At about eleven, Sam took us down to the barn after we had gathered up our sleeping things and tucked our bikes away in the equipment shed near the house. The loft was perfect. One half was full of bales stacked to the rafters; the other half was six inches thick in crackling sweet hay.

We put our sleeping bags in front of the hatchway at the front of the loft Thinking that Sam would now return to the house, we undressed down to our T-shirts and underwear and lay down on top of our bags. Despite the heat and the sweat that dripped from our bodies, making the nylon stick to our skin, we were happy. With our chins propped on elbows, we stared into the dream-like world beyond the hatchway: the barnyard, the big trees, the shed where Little Silver and Big Blue were safely under cover, the stars and the Kentucky sky.

Suddenly we heard Sam coming up the ladder. As nervous and uncomfortable as I was by his unexpected appearance, I thought the whole scene would be less stimulating if we remained calm about our half-naked condition, pretending there was nothing out of the ordinary happening. Sam didn't say a word, and he turned to drop hay down into the stalls below, we slid quickly into our bags. After he finished his chores, he climbed back down the ladder saying, "I'll leave you alone now." All at once, there was a loud banging and thudding down below us in one of the stalls. We could hear Sam cursing and cajoling one of his animals and, after a time, he called up to us that his bull had caught his horns in the rails of his stall and was trapped. Fortunately, the bull wasn't upset about his predicament, and Sam left at a quick trot to bring the tractor to pry the boards off. Carol and I looked at each other in disbelief and dismay—another sleepless night.

The tractor rumbled into the barn, the chain hooked to the boards of the stall, and the bull's horns freed. I peered through the cracks of the floorboards to watch what was going on, sleepily excited by the whole event. Calm fell again over the barn as Sam left to return the tractor to the shed. Soon he returned, presumably to lock up. Not so.

Once again, we heard his steps on the loft ladder; it was too late to jump into our bags. I was immediately suspicious when he started explaining what had been going on downstairs; he had no reason to tell us—least of all in person. I said something dumb like, "Gee, the work of a farmer is never done; I hope this doesn't happen all the time. *Goodnight.*" I hoped my tone of voice would cut off any further conversation.

I was very nervous. He continued to stand on the top rung staring at us. After an interminable moment he said in a matter-of-fact voice, "Do y'all want a companion for the night?" We were too stunned to speak. What was going on? What did he think we were doing besides trying to go to sleep? Did he really think he could take us both on or was he going to pick one of us? I recovered first and stammered, "No, we're just fine, thanks. *Goodnight.*" (Please, mister, just go away!) He returned the "good night" and casually backed down the ladder after a last, lingering gaze.

I was in a cold sweat, tingling all over, my heart pounding furiously. We held our breaths until we heard the barn door close and we saw Sam walk to the house. Would he return in the middle of the night and surprise us? Should we go to sleep? We decided he didn't look that determined or perverse, nor did we feel he could overpower two of us. He looked so simple, so calm, so gentle. What grand perception of himself as a lover did he have? So bold—and at his age! (Yet I couldn't fault him for trying, and his inquiry was made honestly and with dignity.) We lay very still for a long time, looking out the hatchway, searching for a figure stealthily creeping toward the barn. We were both upset, feeling our sexual vulnerability as never before.

After we felt sure he wasn't going to return, we allowed ourselves to be lulled into sleep by the musical munching of cattle eating their supper below us, lowing their pleasure. Before we fell asleep, however, we agreed to leave before light, before anyone was up. We didn't want to deal with such an awkward situation again in the morning.

DAY 53: I woke up off and on as the morning drew closer, looking to see how dark it was, estimating how long it would be before we could travel. At the first hint of light, I woke Carol. She grumbled groggily, but I was wide awake, ready for action. I felt oddly excited, as if I were part of a spy novel.

In the dark, we crept carefully down the ladder with our sleeping bags and all our paraphernalia. God help us if we wake that bull! We tiptoed to the barn door. It had been locked from the outside. I wasn't surprised, but it added considerably to the suspense of our adventure. I managed to slip a thin piece of wire through the crack in the door and lift up the hook. We pushed on the door, gently slowly, waiting for it to creak. Then, quickly, across the barnyard, through another gate and over to the garage, which was directly across from the house. It was 5:30 a.m. when we walked our bikes quietly down the driveway and out onto the road. We mounted and pedaled quickly away. My only unpleasant thoughts came from knowing that the sister left the house at 6:00 to go to work at the factory in Danville—where we were headed—and I wondered what she would think or do if she passed us. We never knew.

Shifts were changing at the factories when we arrived in Danville. A steady stream of cars pulled in and out of the parking lots like an army of ants. I imagined that every one of those workers knew that I was rich and privileged, that somehow, even though I wasn't wearing anything that was expensive, the signs were all there. I had dreaded traveling through the poor parts of the eastern United States. I felt guilty that I would never have to experience poverty and the demanding, tedious, unfulfilling work that these people lived and breathed every day of their lives.

I had spent most of my life hating the wealth I grew up with, that I had inherited and hadn't worked a lick for. Somehow I knew, even at a very early age, that my family's status was an unjust situation. I believed I was different from other people, special, significantly better than the rest of the world. (Linne tells me that rich people protect themselves from suffering too much guilt by explaining to themselves that the reason they have more money than most people is that they are superior and, therefore, justly compensated.) I never had to wait in lines, hotel rooms were always the most elegant, the maitre d' at a fine restaurant would be particularly attentive and solicitous.

I enjoyed this special attention, but felt guilty and embarrassed by it, too. I was a very shy child and tried my hardest to be farthest from the center of attention. There were public occasions when my father would demand certain favors—special treatment he was used to—and I would be mortified to have any connection with him. People would look at him, and then I'd feel them looking at me, hating him and hating me. Since the time I was fourteen, the knowledge that people were envious and jealous of me, my money and my position, had become intolerable.

Sometimes I've wished I had no money at all. When people ask me, "What do you do?" I would give anything to be able to say, "I'm a secretary," or "I teach third grade." Instead, I cringe and tighten up inside, praying that the moment will pass quickly. If I'm "working," I can be just like everybody else, instead of sitting at home writing a book about my bike trip or building a solar natural foods restaurant in suburbia. I leave little room for pleasure or fun in my life because I now feel obligated to earn the money I have, money I didn't deserve in the first place. I've thought about giving it all away, but I know I could never rid myself of it completely. I would always have that element in my background and it would affect the way I am, no matter how poorly I lived. So, I'm learning to live with it, to enjoy it, to put it to constructive uses, to work with it instead of avoid it or pretend it doesn't exist.

In the thick of these tangled emotions, we pulled into Stivey's for breakfast and found ourselves at the counter with a dozen factory workers. We had a fun breakfast. The guys were interested in and impressed by our journey. They gave us good advice about what roads to take. Nonetheless, I was relieved to arrive in Berea, Kentucky, the charming tourist and college town.

We spent a full afternoon in Berea, tending to our laundry—at last—and savoring goodies at the natural food store. The more we saw of Berea, the more we liked it. We browsed in a small socialist bookstore, selecting a book of poems and short stories called *Kentucky Renaissance* to read to each other at night. Neither of us had had the energy to do any reading on the trip and we missed that stimulation.

We visited the college museum which devoted its work to encouraging and supporting a renaissance in the old Appalachian culture and crafts. We carefully watched the slides of the area we would be biking through, noting the weather, estimating the steepness of the mountain grades. We felt better and better as the day wore on, more confident about biking into those unknown mountains. The Appalachians were the last barriers we would have to cross before reaching Washington, DC.

DAY 54: Before leaving Berea, however, we had to face a different sort of challenge. It had long been planned that Arthur would join us for the last seven to ten days of our trip. Carol and I had talked about this from time to time for the past six weeks. I had hesitations about having a new person join us, and fears that the two of them would be so wrapped up with each other that I would be excluded. But I also genuinely felt that Arthur would be fun to have with us, even though I didn't know him. Perhaps Carol and I would be roused into a lighter, more festive mood if we had a fresh biker with us, one who had not just spent the last fifty-three days on the road and who would not be merely trying to finish the trip as we were. However, since seeing "Unmarried Woman" in St. Louis, we had increasingly felt that this was a women's trip—*our* trip—and we would feel especially good to finish it together.

Before breakfast that morning, Carol called Arthur to test the waters, to see how strongly he would react to a repeal of the original invitation. Much to her dismay, she discovered he had been happily bustling around Washington getting his bike and gear ready and was greatly looking forward to his "vacation" bike trip. They agreed to talk again in a couple of days, but in all of our hearts, we knew what the decision would be.

We left Berea in the late morning of a clear, sunny day on June 23rd, after honeydew melon, bran muffins and cream cheese. The good weather was an unexpected pleasure and we biked at a good pace along the country roads. Carol was having a hard time though, debating with herself what to do about Arthur. She felt empty and depressed. I tried to help her sort out the conflicts and emotions, offering my own thoughts when she wanted them. Eventually, she came to believe most strongly that it was the right thing for us to finish the trip together alone.

In the late afternoon, a roadside pay phone appeared at the side of an untraveled road at just the time Carol told Arthur she would call. His anger from that morning had turned to an understanding of how important it was for us to finish the trip by ourselves. They arranged a sailing trip to compensate for the missed bicycle adventure. She was teary when she hung up, so we sat for a while, I reassured her that it was okay to do what she had done, that we had to be good to ourselves; to do what felt right to us. Soon, we were congratulating ourselves on the decision and agreed that from then on we would *celebrate* the last stage of our journey instead of feeling we had to get through it as soon as possible. We agreed to spend more nights in motels and find treats wherever possible.

Much to my disappointment, we did not find a motel that night. On top of that, when we stopped at a house outside Campton, the man who answered the door hardly bothered to look at us, keeping his eyes carefully averted as he pointed out a camping spot on his lawn. I couldn't understand what was wrong. Somehow, I sensed it related to the noticeable increase in the amount of cat-calling and hooting that we attracted from passing cars over the past hundred miles or so. Irritating honking, stares and attention. That afternoon, I had felt particularly victimized; each honk pierced into me, each hoot was like a claw tearing my flesh. I felt totally worthless and humiliated. When two unsuspecting road workers said something cute to us about the hill we were climbing, I decided to fight back. To their surprise and my pleasure, I snapped, "We've come from California and we'll get over this ant hill, too!" By the look on their faces, I knew they'd been properly snubbed.

Despite regaining a sense of strength, I was apprehensive that night, both from the cold reception from our host and from knowing we were about to get into some really steep country. My same old fears about whether or not I could do it were coming up. I tried valiantly to squash my doubts with positive "yes I can" feelings. It was a titanic battle of intergalactic proportions. By the time I went to sleep, however, the forces of good had pulled slightly into the lead.

DAY 55: Much to our surprise and delight, the terrain was not as bad as we'd expected. Granted, we ran into a few formidable hills, but nothing as difficult or strenuous as those we'd found in the Ozarks. Instead, we threaded our way along a winding country road through the foothill country of the Appalachians. Of course, I had a flat tire—sometimes it seemed as if we couldn't make it through a whole day without some hang-up or other. I was grateful that it happened near an old tobacco barn; I didn't relish changing my tire by the side of the road where we'd surely be the center of attention for honkers and hooters.

We were so engrossed in our work that we scarcely noticed the old man who walked silently into the barn and sat on a hay bale to watch us. He seemed quite fascinated by the whole thing, but his piercing gaze made us nervous. Was he going to yell at us, kick us out or attack?

Finally he spoke. We were so startled by his "foreign" language that it was several seconds before we could respond. His dialect was so strong and so far removed from the English we spoke, that it took every bit of concentration to understand his general meaning.

He seemed friendly—fortunately, since it turned out to be his barn—and asked a few questions. He was clearly puzzled by us. He asked us both if we were married. When Carol replied no, he asked if she were looking for a husband. She laughed and explained our adventure, but he didn't seem to understand. As we rode away, we decided that he must have thought Carol was touring the country in search of a suitable man to marry. Since I was already attached, we could only surmise that he thought I was a whore. Our worlds were decades apart. I was shocked and fascinated that such contrast existed in our country, thrilled to be witnessing—no, experiencing—this phenomenon.

The country became poorer and poorer as we neared the West Virginia border. Houses became shacks, barns were mere illusions of a wood frame shelter. Most places had small gardens, the family's most precious possession. All were growing substantial quantities of tobacco. There was something very maudlin about that.

In West Liberty, about midday, we stopped for some fresh grapes. As we biked out of town, we were hailed by a young man on the side of the road. He told us he was a biker and a runner—an anomaly in these parts—and was eager to hear about our trip. We compared athletic notes for a while and then he directed us out of town. To make sure we'd found the right route, he drove ahead to wait for us at the crossroads and waved us out of sight.

The road remained pleasant, following the foothills, but it was hot and humid. By the time we reached Blaire, fourteen miles from our night's destination, it was still 86° at 4:00 in the afternoon. Still, we had no anxieties about reaching Louisa with ease, having been encouraged by the gentle terrain we'd just biked through. We were doubly confident when the woman we asked at the grocery store told us the route ahead was not at all hilly.

After 3000 miles, we should have learned a lesson about not having any expectations about what lay ahead. Our second mistake was to ask someone else to confirm those expectations, and to believe her perceptions would be the same as our own. We were the only ones who felt every roll in the terrain, every incline, every pothole to bump and crash over. When we came to the chuck holes, the rocks and the steep grades outside Blaire, we were incensed. The woman had obviously lied to us about the road. Despite our indignant accusations, we knew full well it was our own fault that we were so miserable; we would have been better off not asking.

We dragged into Louisa tired and bitchy. We crossed the bridge into West Virginia for a legal can of cold beer, then returned to the Best Western Motel. The manager helped us haul our bikes up to the second floor, and we settled into our room for dinner and a night of television. We were growing more and more tired of the trip, physically and mentally. But we'd crossed another state line; it wouldn't be long anymore.

DAY 56: I awoke as depressed and gloomy as I'd been the night before, and bored with feeling that way. I tried to rouse my spirits by talking with Carol while we biked and then singing for a while. I also decided to try a different and radical biking technique—setting my own pace instead of trying to keep up with Carol. In this hilly country, she could easily out-do me with her hill-climbing ability. I would find myself frantically trying to keep up with her, which I could usually do but at some cost to my nerves and energy. I would quickly do myself in if I didn't change that pattern, so I set my mind to my own body, my own rhythm, switching gears as I felt the need.

For the first time in fifty-five days, I believed there was no better or worse in biking faster or slower; indeed, there was no such thing. No useful value could be placed on our difference in paces. (Was I rationalizing my falling behind?) I was okay, my pace was okay, my body was okay, Carol was okay. I felt a sublime sense of wellness, as though a heavy shell had been lifted off my body. I could hardly wait to tell Carol about my revelation—as soon as I caught up with her.

Despite that happy sense of freedom, I began to feel physically run down. At times, climbing a steep grade, I felt as if I were in my own private sauna bath; the sweat poured off me like an open faucet, and I burned all over. By the time we reached Sod, sixty-six miles from Louisa, I was completely burned out. I was so low on energy I was unable to decide what I wanted to do.

I felt horribly inadequate at not being able to finish the day's ride. My body had let me down. Could it be that I wasn't superhuman after all? My physical and emotional weakness was aggravated by our being completely out of water for the first time in our entire journey. I sat propped against the grubby stucco wall of the deserted gas station in Sod, hoping someone would pull in and offer to take us the rest of the way to Charleston—or Washington, for that matter. When it didn't happen, we got on our bikes to ride to the grocery store we were told was at the bottom of the next hill. Thank God, it was. After taking one gulp of the local water, however, we knew we had to hitch a ride out. It was the most vile, ghastly tasting liquid I have ever drunk, worse than Kaopectate. The foul water was matched by the polluted air. I learned later that Charleston is one of the leading areas in the country for chemical pollution—such an honor. If I'd known that bit of trivia at the time, I'm sure it would have killed me.

With hopeful thumbs and discouraged hearts, we sat ourselves and our bikes by the side of the road and waited. Shortly, a battered blue sedan pulled up, and a young man asked if we wanted to ride with him. At first, I thought to send him on since it wasn't a pickup, but Carol persuaded me to accept the ride while we had a chance. We managed to cram all our gear and bikes into the trunk and backseat, and the three of us squeezed into the front.

Jimmy, our chauffeur, was a quiet, baby-faced, beer-drinking construction worker on his way to South Charleston. He was shy and we talked little. I was nervous about all the beer he was drinking (or rather, my mother was nervous about it), but he seemed to be driving all right. We accepted his offer to take us through Charleston. When we saw the extent of the interchanges and construction areas we were deeply grateful for the lift.

For all his youthful appearance and manner, Jimmy was married and the father of three children. He proudly showed us a picture of the baby. He said he would take us to a motel he knew of outside Charleston. I felt totally at his mercy, yet trusting and completely happy for such a long and unexpected ride. He could very easily have kept going to Washington for all the half-hearted resistance we put up as mile after mile slipped by.

Eventually, we arrived at the motel in Clendenin. As if he hadn't already saved the day for us, Jimmy took us to the grocery store down the road so we could pick up some dinner and drove us back. He had taken us sixteen miles out of his way. We bought a six-pack of beer at the market and left it in the back of his car.

Despite our good fortune, I was sullen and quiet that night, and Carol had to push me before I confided what was bothering me. I was ashamed of being so exhausted, so in need of help. I had never seen myself in such a physically pitiful condition; I detested such weakness in myself. Upon reflection, I realized the incident harkened back to trying desperately and mightily to please my father, to win his attention and affection by performing Herculean tasks. Linne had said to me before I left that I should observe myself if I ever had to ask for help—as if she knew something I didn't. I needed Carol's reassurance that she didn't think less of me because I'd been so weak. She thought the whole idea was ridiculous, but was quick to reassure me that I hadn't shattered any grand images she had of me.

DAY 57: We got off to a good start, rejuvenated by the big jump we'd made by car. Our route—shady and flat—led us along the Elk River Scenic Drive, bordered on one side by the wide muddy Elk River and on the other side by a lush dense forest. The mornings were the most enjoyable times of the day; the air cool and dewy, the sun still a pale glow filtering through the trees. It never stayed that way long enough; soon we were dripping great quantities of sweat, as though we were taking showers from the inside out. We stopped before noon at a tiny general store, searching the shelves for just the right snack. After finding no fresh fruit whatsoever, our eyes fixed on pretzels, molasses cookies, and strawberry ice cream sundaes. For some weird reason, the combination hit the spot. We felt like naughty children, sheepish about enjoying our junk food so much, sucking with delight on the little white plastic spoons until there was no strawberry flavor left.

We arrived in Duck—about as wet as one—for lunch. We collapsed inside a small, air-conditioned store, where the owner, an attractive woman in her mid-thirties, offered us lunch. We declined Iona Legg's steak sandwiches, explaining we were vegetarians. Her eyes lit up and she ushered us into her living room at the back of the store, where she cut up a cantaloupe melon, set her table with homemade whole-grain bread, almond butter and comb honey. She offered us a shower and a place to spend the night, an invitation we would have accepted if we hadn't wanted to make many more miles before the end of the day. After lunch she filled our bottles with ice water and bid us goodbye.

That afternoon, I was suddenly struck with the idea of writing about the trip, something that hadn't occurred to me until then. I thought of how I would put together a portfolio of pictures with stories suitable for different magazines, of how to advertise and distribute the articles. It sounded like fun and a good way to keep the trip alive after we had finished. Besides, I wanted to read Carol's journal, and she mine. We fantasized and talked eagerly about it for the rest of the day.

We stopped for the night in an ultra-modern interstate motel and thoroughly enjoyed the comfort of a genuine working air-conditioner; as usual, the heat was unbearable and we were a sticky mess. An enormous lightning and thunder storm came up in the early evening. The rain came down in torrents, and the wind blew with gale force. We stared out the window, as if cast under a spell by the power and force of the storm. We enjoyed its magnificence even more when we thought of how little rain we'd had on the trip. I called Tony that night, as usual, and I could tell from his voice that he was starting to get excited, too. The end was in sight.

DAY 58: I don't know why I started thinking about laws of physics that morning, but within a few miles of the motel, I was absorbed in the First and Second Laws of Thermodynamics. These bewildering principles—that the energy in the world is constant and merely changes form and that order tends toward disorder—had always taken an enormous effort to understand. Now, as a result of my bicycle travels, they were becoming clear. Bicycle parts dry out, cake with grit and grease, and become unworkable unless a certain amount of time is spent cleaning and oiling, listening to the bike's humming, watching its condition and tending to its needs. The same concept applied to me. Without constant vigilance, I slip into familiar patterns: stop looking after my health, gorge on ice cream, get lazy about exercising, stop trying. My reflections continued, moving from physics to geography, mercifully diverting my attention from how hot and muggy it was becoming.

As we approached the Appalachian Mountains, the foothills were giving us plenty of build-up for what was ahead. As we rode over a series of steep ups and downs in the easterly direction and then gradual soft terrain in the northerly direction, we began to see ourselves as tiny ants traveling over a series of bumps as we crossed the grain of the land, and then easily moving up the swales. All across America, we'd discovered patterns in the terrain. Short foothills built up to mountains; a steep descent resolved to a perfectly flat plain below; undulating hills became steeper and shorter in their rises and falls. We could have built a three-dimensional model of the country we had passed through. It was exciting to have that perception of the earth, the understanding that came from actually moving our bodies over it, as a blind person might lightly feel the contours and features of a person she meets, translating touch into an image. Before the steepness of the hills jarred me from my reverie, I thought, somewhat wistfully, that the world is a school. Gladly would I have traded fourteen years of sitting in a dull classroom for a few bicycle trips.

As we crossed over hills and rode up valleys, our anxiety about the Appalachians increased. That morning, a construction worker on the road had glibly exclaimed to us, "Just wait 'til you hit the *real* mountains tomorrow!" We knew nothing about them, and since we were already working pretty hard in this terrain, we envisioned the worst.

That morning's forty-eight miles left us collapsed on a bench under the eaves of a small store, gulping cold drinks and cooling our tongues on ice cream. If this was any indication of what was coming, we had good reason to be anxious. The owner of the store offered us the use of the bathroom in his house across the way. I went off to use the facilities and left my wallet lying on the bench. While I was sitting on the john, Carol came in with the wallet and reprimanded me for being so careless. I thanked her, but insisted that I didn't want to be treated like a child, which I felt she was doing We didn't speak about it anymore, but on the road again, I noticed she was riding farther ahead than usual and biking particularly hard.

When I finally caught up with her in Buchanan, she looked very serious and said she had a heavy thought to share with me. (Oh great!) She explained why she'd been biking so hard. She was angry that the uneven distribution of wealth in this country permitted me the freedom of leaving my wallet in public, while other people had to scrounge and slave to make enough to exist. I felt very threatened. Would this be the thing that would ruin our friendship? As much as I didn't want to ask, I had to find out if she resented me for my money and if she could never fully accept me because of it. At such a crucial point in our developing friendship, I wondered whether she would even admit those feelings if she had them. I risked the question. No, she said, she didn't hate me because I was rich, and went on to say that anyone who suffered as much guilt as I did from having more than a fair share of money didn't need to be punished further. I listened to her silently. The incident upset me too much, raised too many fears, to be easily dismissed or resolved. Despite her efforts to reassure me, my mood was sullen as we rode the next few miles in search of the local swimming pool.

It was difficult to discern whether there was any water in the pool for all the people who were packed in it like so many sardines. We managed to stake out a small area in which to dunk ourselves to soothe our strained nerves and rinse the sweat off our bodies. Most of the tension fell away as we ate our lunch by the pool and, map spread out, contemplated the next thirty miles to Elkins, gateway to the Appalachians.

Every time we stopped, no matter how short the time, we studied our maps. We would look not only at the upcoming route, but also at the area near and far from where we were, finding the names of places we knew, estimating miles, imagining the span of the mountain range, calculating distances we could make, admiring the distance we'd come. The maps, with their many folds and creases, were an endless source of pleasure, relaxation and information.

We assumed the terrain to Elkins would be steep. We also assumed we'd run into coal trucks. We'd been fortunate to have avoided them so far, but we were about to travel on one of their primary routes. Moreover, there were no towns between our swimming pool and Elkins—a depressing situation since we knew we would want to shower that night after such a grueling day. To keep from slipping into low spirits, we agreed to bike only as far as we could, and then hitch the rest of the way to Elkins.

The road was worse than we'd imagined. The climb was long and steep, the weather was at its hottest and muggiest. Drivers would bring their cars to within a few feet of our rear wheels, then lean on their horns. We held our ground, preferring angry motorists to being run off the road. The coal trucks, while respectful of our space on the road, were abundant and belched black fumes as they climbed slowly up the grade. The only things to breathe were exhaust and humidity. Somehow, despite my dull headache, we kept going. When we reached the summit, we had only a few, much easier miles to Elkins.

We staggered into a bar, embarrassed by the flow of sweat we brought with us, and ordered several Country Lemonade drinks which were treacle sweet but cold and refreshing. Truckers there were amazed—so were we. We hadn't expected to make it as far as we did and, by God, we had made it by pedal power! Despite feeling physically done in, our spirits and pride were soaring high, our hearts full of a sense of accomplishment and strength. With great satisfaction, I watched the grit pour off me that night in the shower.

DAY 59: We set out in the morning to conquer "five mountains in thirty-five miles." That was the word we got from locals in the Elkins cafe where we had breakfast. We were both nervous—even to the point of admitting it—not knowing what to expect up ahead, not knowing if we'd be able to get over those mountains. A true San Francisco fog—rich, thick, gray wetness—added to the mystery and anticipation. It was, indeed, one mountain after another. The grades ranged from long, steady uphills to shorter, very steep climbs. It wasn't until our assault on the second mountain that the fog lifted and we were able to see that we were in the heart of the

Appalachian Mountains. They were thickly forested; trees dripped with dew above delicately patterned ferns on the forest floor below. The smells and sounds were as lush as the forest.

As we climbed the fifth mountain, the air filled with an eerie, rhythmic, high-pitched whine which totally surrounded us. I fully expected to see my first UFO or find out that this was the site of secret CIA operations. We continued our ascent and the unearthly vibrations continued. Eventually I realized that the sound was actually coming from the forest insects; a chorus of millions, they sang the strangest music I have ever heard.

Our fifth mountain ended at the Mouth of Seneca—one of the most romantic place names we'd come across. The weather had turned absolutely sparkling for the first time in many days. Patches of electric blue sky parted the fog and clouds, and our spirits rose to greet the sun. We rested at the grocery store, relieved to have met the challenge and still be alive to tell the tale. We felt even better about ourselves when we met two young men bike tourists who looked as if they'd just been run over by a coal truck. They'd started in Illinois and were headed, as we were, to Washington. They had had bad luck all the way. They'd been blown off the road by a truck, suffered a twisted wheel, broken spokes, and had had no shower for days. Their spirits were so low we could have stepped over them.

I was suddenly struck with an idea. I took the tassel from my bike and found the bag of peppermint tea. I put them together in Gerry's box together with a lucky dime, and our goodwill and blessings, and presented it to them. They were cheered and touched by the gift; I felt wonderfully inspired. My gift was one of hope and courage, coming from one who was fulfilled to those who were in need. They took our photograph, and we left, counting our blessings as we wound our way along the Potomac. Tomorrow, I thought with a deep welling in my chest, my T-shirt saying "California to Virginia" would be true.

DAY 60: Our second-to-last morning! We set out into a clear and sunny June twenty-ninth stoked with buckwheat cakes and lots of excitement. The owners at the cafe marveled at our adventure. People we met no longer gave us patronizing looks and said, "Oh, you've got a long way to go." Even as far east as Kentucky, folks never said, "Wow, you've come a long way." They always said, "Boy, you've got a lot of miles ahead of you." Now it was, "Well, you're not far now." We were starting to realize that ourselves.

Long before the Mouth of Seneca, Carol had found the clarity and courage to decide that she wanted to find a new job in Washington, DC. She was making arrangements for interviews upon our arrival, stopping periodically to make phone calls at an appointed hour. It was strange to be planning for the end of the trip, for lives beyond what we had known for the last two months.

We climbed a couple of good-sized mountains in the morning, one that was four and a half miles up, and then—ta da!—four and a half miles down. How high it was! The last grand descent couldn't have been more dramatic and exhilarating. It seemed never to end. We flew through sparkling forest, the leaves of the trees shimmering and fluttering in a light breeze, through clean pure air. It was a joy to fill my lungs with its goodness.

That early morning ride unveiled a surprise beyond any expectations or dreams I had ever had about the trip. I had been singing exuberantly all morning, going through the repertoire of songs I had built up mile after mile through the monotonous stretches of Eastern Colorado and Kansas. Suddenly, I began to listen to myself. A change had taken place. My voice, far from being hesitant and small as it had been for so long, was—well—beautiful. The tone was rich and full of feeling; the melodies came from somewhere deep within me, hitting the notes clearly and confidently. I was flabbergasted. I didn't kid myself that it was a voice that would get me to the Grand Old Opry, but it was a hell of an improvement since last I'd heard it. Could pedaling 3,500 miles work such wonders? What would happen if I went around the world? I felt very choked up inside. Tears were in my eyes as we crossed the border into Virginia.

That afternoon we arrived in Front Royal, Virginia, seventy miles from Washington. We were delighted with our dinner selection—Brie, Port Salut, Gruyere cheese, Carr's crackers and a good red wine—but also sadly aware of what the availability of these gourmet treats meant. Civilization was close by; the end was here. In a daze of excitement and sadness we found a motel, and Carol made a final call to Arthur to plan a route into the city and arrange our rendezvous.

We were not particularly happy knowing that the salad we were eating while sitting on the floor of our motel room would be our last. Everything we did that night was our "last": the last bottle of wine, the last call home from the road, the last night we'd share a motel room in just this way. It was with a mixture of sadness and elation that we talked that night about the trip, about each other, about what we would be doing after it was over. We shared some of the things we'd observed about each other, the patterns and habits we thought it would help to talk about. They were not new thoughts—we'd shared just about everything as we went along: how Carol was always apologizing, assuming that any mistake was completely her fault; how I was always doing everything by myself, not asking for help. (It had taken almost the whole trip for me to be willing to ask Carol during short stops on the road to hold my bike while I peed.)

But there was one thing we hadn't discussed. Carol had pointed out to me a few days before that whenever people asked about us, I would always explain that I was married, and sometimes I'd add that Carol was not. The tone of my voice and the way I phrased it made it sound as if *I* were acceptable and Carol was not. It reflected a deep belief I held onto about women: that she who is not attached to a man is not whole, not complete. Intellectually, I completely reject this belief. I fully support *any* woman who doesn't want to get married, who is independent and free of that attachment. God knows there have been more than a few times when I wished to be that way myself. Yet I was taught by my mother and by the culture that a woman is nowhere without a man, that her main purpose in life—her only protection, in fact—is to find a man, marry, and devote the rest of her life to her husband. The worst thing a woman can do is jeopardize that security. To take a two month leave of absence for a bicycle trip clearly falls in the category of insanity.

A close friend of my mother was aghast when I told her of my trip, saying she would never *dream* of leaving her husband alone for such a long time. Women in my mother's generation were quite helpless as single women—at least they thought they were. It was beyond their imagination that I should take such a risk for my own pleasure and fulfillment. I was taken aback when Carol challenged me about this. I do not like to think of myself as having sexist beliefs. Like the dregs of a fine wine, those ideas linger and settle and sometimes slip unnoticed into the last glass.

DAY 61: The morning of June thirtieth passed much like any other. The day was blessedly clear and sunny. We rode through mostly flat farm country for about forty miles, now in open fields, now through patches of forest. And then, suddenly, there it was—civilization. A 747 roared over our heads, dumping black exhaust fumes on us as though we were tomatoes being sprayed with herbicide. We were startled and frightened. We had entered a forgotten world, a world of noise, pollution, traffic, shopping centers and city life. They had all been obliterated from our lives for eight and a half weeks, and we had adjusted happily to living without them.

We approached Washington with sadness, joy, nervousness, confidence, trepidation and pride. Depression fell over us like a soggy warm blanket. I was surprised, because I had expected to feel ecstatic. Fortunately, the circumstances did not permit us to dwell on our confusion. About twenty miles from the center of the city, we made a wrong turn. After many miles of searching for the right route, and at wit's end, we stopped at a commercial building to ask directions. It was the local animal control shelter. What a perfect test, I thought morbidly. Perhaps because I was lost myself, I was not overcome by the desire to take home any lost puppies.

Once on the right road, we were the object of verbal abuse all the way through suburbia—Reston, Alexandria, Falls Church. "Sex, sex!" "Hiya, Baby," they cried from their cars. A harder challenge for our journey's end we could not have picked. We even had to go over a stretch of gravel road!

We stopped on the Key Bridge to stare at the Washington Monument and the Potomac River—and to take our twelfth picture without film, realizing with dismay that the camera had been empty since the border. We arrived at Lincoln Memorial at 5:00 p.m., exhausted. It was a dramatic ending.

Unfortunately, there was no chance to sit and reflect on the historic moment; it was gnat season at the Memorial, and only constant waving and fanning held off the swarms of little, black buzzing creatures. Arthur arrived in his VW van and whisked us off to a lovely three-story Washington townhouse which he was housesitting. Carol and I were spacey and tired. I was greatly relieved that Arthur was there to take care of us. All that l recall is going to dinner at a little French restaurant where I had a strawberry tart for dessert. A long sleep followed, no reason to rush off in the morning.

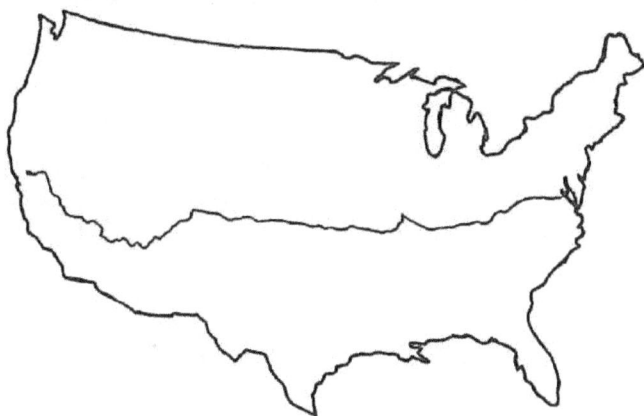

The Ending

I haven't the courage to keep tramping forever without getting anywhere at all.

JULY 3: WASHINGTON, DC—Now two full days off the bikes; seems strange and I'm in a daze at times. It's been raining. Must be making up for only three wet biking miles on the road.

Feel the need to put down my roots again and I look forward to meeting Tony in Michigan. The time we've been in DC feels like an extension of the trip. I see myself doing, saying, behaving differently—with more assurance, confidence and clarity. For instance, last night we were at a bar in the Holiday Inn after visiting Carol's parents. I persuaded Carol to dance with me, and when Arthur cut in, I needed my own partner so I could keep dancing. So I asked a man who was sitting at the bar to join me. After a couple of dances, I turned to him and said, "Thank you, I enjoyed that very much." He returned to the bar. I watched myself as if I had stepped out of my body and were viewing the scene from above. Where had I gotten the guts to do that?

Too much liquor and food in the last two days. Getting too far away from my body. Had a dream last night that was filled with self-destructive images.

Such a nice day with Carol, the first time in two that we've been by ourselves. I drove her to a job interview—I felt as if it were *our* interview. Packed off Little Silver this morning. It was like watching surgery on my best friend. The box was small, and an incompetent guy was trying to figure out how to fit it in. I watched the operation through a little glass window as he fumbled and struggled, jammed and twisted the bike into the box. For this I paid ten dollars.

Saw my old friend Joy last night; a warm and intimate evening. It was great to get back together again. She was full of praise for my journey. Washington is like a zoo now with hordes of tourists. We may never get to the National Gallery. Oh, well.

JULY 5: WEQUETONSING, MICHIGAN—A few withdrawal and re-entry pains for Tony and me.

I cried at landing safely at the Pellston Airport. As I envisioned, Tony was there in his red-checkered Vyella shirt and khaki pants. We hugged closely and a little self-consciously. His family was very glad to see me, hugs and kisses all around. Tony's mother has been exceedingly open and warm to me this visit, even to the point of good-naturedly teasing me the other night. First time I've felt accepted by her in ten years. Perhaps the trip has given me more legitimacy in her eyes. At last.

Tony became sullen during pre-dinner festivities, and as we sat in bed later that night, he confided he felt ambivalent about my suddenly being back. I asked him what *he* had liked about being alone. "No pressure, doing things on my own time, doing what I wanted to do." One joy of the trip for me was being free of responsibilities of house, bills, animals, doing exactly what I loved to do, and not having to worry about what Tony wanted or needed. After we talked, we went out to the hammock in the front yard and made love. I was very horny, open and unafraid.

JULY 6: WEQUETONSING—I had a compelling and insatiable urge to *buy.* We went to Petoskey, high class shopping area, and I managed with great difficulty to restrain myself to buying one dressy T-shirt, a pair of shoes and a leather purse. In spite of my self-restraint, we spent money on this and that all morning long—not the best image of myself, but I decided to indulge the urge.

We'd decided—mutually, I thought—to make dinner for Helen and Jim at their house—buckwheat crepes stuffed with mushrooms, Bluff Garden carrots and beets, and my special dried fruit pie. Our best. Tony and I struggled over whether to have a spinach salad as well as spinach in the crepe filling. I tried to adjust to the reality that shopping with Tony was not as pleasant and easy as shopping with Carol. Carol and I would have opted for the salad. Tony was impatient to return to the beach. Food was so important to Carol and me; why not to him?

Walking to the Point, to sister Lucy's house where we were staying, my right leg began to ache from no exercise, and by the time I sat down alone at the piano, I was desperately missing Carol, missing our trip, our mutual and easy understanding of one another, feeling sluggish and overfed, wishing not to be *here.* I fluctuated for a few moments between staying inside, alone with my misery, or going outside to the beach to talk about it with Tony. How could I tell him I wanted to be with Carol instead of him? Finally, feeling that I no longer wanted to bear my problems alone, I went out to share them.

I had anticipated and dreaded Tony's reaction: "Oh, fuck! Do I have to deal with *your* problems? Can't I have a couple of days of peace and quiet on the beach, with no dinners to cook, no tears to deal with?" Oh, if *only* I could get back to Carol!

We hung on together, trying to find the right words, the way to reach each other. Tony confessed he was anxious about going back to work and that he was tired of Michigan's constant barrage of social activity and chatter. In his best histrionic stage form, he pleaded with me to have a little sympathy for *him*. "Show a little milk of human kindness," he begged. "Bullshit!" I snapped. Nobody can tell me I'm not a kind person. Eventually, we struggled to the end of the scene, feeling better for it. I was happy not to be overcome with guilt about interrupting him and falling apart. I knew I'd done the right thing to talk about how I was feeling, but sometimes I wonder what the big attraction is for couples to be "open" with each other.

We made—together—a terrifically delicious and successful dinner. Tony later confided how much he'd enjoyed the day, despite our struggle.

JULY 7: WEQUETONSING—I'm tired of sleeping in a different bed every night, of having such limited choices of food. I'm in a fog. I feel "grown up," but unreal. Who is me that is feeling and being who I am? Who cries and curses and talks back? Who stands up for herself, doesn't run away, makes her desires known, asks for what she wants? Is this still me? And who is me? Pooh Bear?

Got up without waiting as usual for Tony and went for tea and to write in my journal on the porch. Last night we rode home on an old tandem bike. Tony said it was a little like our marriage, tricky to steer, needs extra energy to pump uphill and balancing in the rear when it wobbles. But when we were cruising, the pleasure and fun of it was immeasurable.

On a lone walk along the beach—Tony was still asleep—I discovered this thought: the reason I run away—stay alone—is to become "lost"; and the reason I want to be "lost" is so that I can be "found." And what I get from being "found" is that it proves to me that someone cares enough about me to look for me. Do I need that anymore? Have I found me enough not to worry about other people finding me? And can I now go to other people and tell them that I need to be cared for, instead of relying on their sensitivity and perception to notice I need help? That seems to be asking an awful lot of people, to read my mind and feelings and interpret my needs. I *can* do it myself. I can defend myself, protect myself. Isn't that the ultimate goal of self-sufficiency?

JULY 8: AMERICAN AIRLINES—Midday, on the way home. Flying at 28,000 feet and 500 mph, I find myself intently studying the country: the landscape, roads, towns, distances, weather. I wish I had my *map* with me. How can I travel anywhere without my map? I notice everything. What a different perspective! I imagine to myself there's a road we'd be on, there's a town we might have biked through. In four hours we are arriving in San Francisco.

I am nervous, excited, relieved and apprehensive. Going home at last. How will I fit in? How will I be received? Is everything okay? How will I react? Will my friends and the dogs recognize me? I feel as if I've been gone for several years. The changes within me will now be revealed and exercised in the context of my former life in Alamo.

JULY 11: HOME—Stiff creaking knees and sore calves. Trying to attribute meaning to experience. Still confused, spacey, disjointed feelings.

My first day "out" was Sunday at the San Francisco Marathon where Paula was doing her first twenty-six mile race. I cried when I saw her loping down the twenty-second mile stretch. We hugged and she seemed as overjoyed as I at our reunion. I was surprised at how strong my happiness was at seeing her. She hadn't felt *that* important to me when I left. I was elated to finally locate Tom as well, a familiar loving face in a sea of strangers. Found. Separation from friends has made me appreciate their value and importance in life.

JULY 12: HOME—This morning I was feeling more confused and disoriented than ever. I started reading a magazine called "Synthesis" to help me sort things out. Perhaps my uneasiness was because Little Silver was at the bike shop being reassembled that morning. It had become such a vital part of my existence that I'm sure I will feel more together when it is. Wrote a long letter to Carol. Funny how so many things remind me of her, like a postcard that says, "Oh Wow!"

I find myself more inclined to analyze a problem such as how to fix the squeaky refrigerator motor, how best to capture loose chickens. Surely this comes from the need on the trip to be objective, rational, and cool about problems, to analyze before acting.

I have been relaxing on the porch, sunning, reading periodically, feeling guilty for the luxury of that precious time and space. Many insights about how I feel about the trip come to mind: I am open and boastful about my trip because I am immensely proud, and I enjoy the praise, admiration and recognition. At the same time, I am shy and reserved to speak of it because I don't want people to envy me or feel inferior and hence not like me. I don't want to attract too much attention. I also feel inspirational, yet I am afraid of my success as well as my failure. I am struck by these mixed feelings. I'll have to reconcile them somehow.

My accomplishment shows me that there are no limitations to what I can do. It gives me, in my own eyes (and maybe in other people's?) less room for failure. What are my expectations of myself now? What do I have to do next? Do I need to prove myself? To whom? What for?

Many of my old fears have left me, particularly those relating to people. We were met with so much kindness and generosity on our trip and so little unpleasantness or hostility that I begin to believe that my basic distrust and suspicions of people were all wrong, a complete misperception of how people really are. People *never* threatened or endangered our lives. Our co-existence with cars and trucks proved the most dangerous part of the journey. Yet people are so fearful of strangers and of the world, convinced that the country is full of crazy people who randomly murder, rape and brutalize others. And who can blame people for thinking that? The media reports very little else! Perverted criminals generally make bigger headlines than global news. The radio, television and newspapers are full of horror stories, and so we become more and more suspicious, more and more withdrawn and fearful.

But it's not like that. I feel such rage at the media for this deception, this manipulation of events in order to sell copy. They have us believing that criminals are over-running the country, and that's a lie. What is to become of us if we stop believing in the goodness of people?

On October seventh, Carol left for a new life and job in Washington, DC. A part of my life, a part of me, left the same day. No more weekend rides, no overnights at our house before the "century" rides, no breakfasts at the local cafe where we could relive our trip with blueberry pancakes and homemade biscuits almost as good as the ones in Pahrump. No more evenings when the three of us—Tony, Carol and Gibi—

would go out on the town and feel as if we were at Lake Mead or in Westcliffe.

About two weeks before she left, Carol and I went out for a fancy farewell dinner at Trader Vic's. Carol had told me over the phone that she had some heavy thoughts to tell me—not *those* things again!—but I made her wait to tell me until we were settled with our rum drinks in the Polynesian Paradise.

The previous month, we had ridden in our first "century" ride, a hundred-mile tour in one day. Carol had taken a wrong turn and we became separated. I thought she was still ahead of me. Even though we had agreed to stay together, I figured she had changed her mind and was exuberantly flying over hill and dale, loving riding alone, as I was. That was all right with me and I continued on. Actually, she had waited at both check points for me to show up. When she learned at one stop that I had gone on, she was furious. She told me she felt I'd planned it that way, that I had wanted to beat her and so had not waited. I had told her what I thought had happened when we met at the end of the tour. Apparently she blocked it out and had been carrying it all this time, and she had to talk about it. She was relieved to hear my side of the story and we went on to the second heavy thought.

During the last few weeks she felt I resented her for not being available when I wanted her. I wasn't surprised to hear this because it was true. I was uncomfortably aware that I had been cutting off our phone conversations a bit abruptly. I started to cry because I knew what I was doing; I was trying to close her off before she did it to me. I couldn't bear the thought of her leaving. Just talking to her on the phone had made me cry. It was like the time when I was little and I locked my beloved nanny in the bathroom so she couldn't leave on her day off.

Through the tears I tried to explain. She looked me right in the eye and said, "Gibi, you can't do that! You're my friend. You're too important to me to let you close me out like that." I was startled. No one had ever challenged me like that before. She had jammed her foot in the door before I could close it, before I could lock myself off from the world, from hurt and despair, from joy and pleasure, forever and ever.

My journey along the Yellow Brick Road did not end after 3,500 miles. Yet Carol's departure marked the end of a significant chapter. How often I marveled at how we were drawn together for this adventure, and how alike we were. It was as if I'd gone on a cross-country bicycle trip with myself. In growing to love Carol, I'd learned to love myself.

I'd also proved myself to myself. The trip was a way for me to accomplish something *big,* something so clearly terrific that, in being true to myself, I could no longer continue to think of myself as useless and worthless. Crossing America on the Yellow Brick Road was a quest. It was not a "fun" trip. It was not a vacation. It only changed my life.

www.ingramcontent.com/pod-product-compliance
Lightning Source LLC
Chambersburg PA
CBHW021404090426
42742CB00009B/1003